crossing**myself**

crossing**myself**

A STORY OF SPIRITUAL REBIRTH

Greg Garrett

NAVPRESS®

BRINGING TRUTH TO LIFE

OUR GUARANTEE TO YOU

We believe so strongly in the message of our books that we are making this quality guarantee to you. If for any reason you are disappointed with the content of this book, return the title page to us with your name and address and we will refund to you the list price of the book. To help us serve you better, please briefly describe why you were disappointed. Mail your refund request to: NavPress, P.O. Box 35002, Colorado Springs, CO 80935.

The Navigators is an international Christian organization. Our mission is to advance the gospel of Jesus and His kingdom into the nations through spiritual generations of laborers living and discipling among the lost. We see a vital movement of the gospel, fueled by prevailing prayer, flowing freely through relational networks and out into the nations where workers for the kingdom are next door to everywhere.

NavPress is the publishing ministry of The Navigators. The mission of NavPress is to reach, disciple, and equip people to know Christ and make Him known by publishing life-related materials that are biblically rooted and culturally relevant. Our vision is to stimulate spiritual transformation through every product we publish.

ISBN 1-57683-856-0

Cover design by Charles Brock/www.thedesignworksgroup.com
Cover image by imagestate.com
Creative Team: Terry Behimer, Don Simpson, Darla Hightower, Arvid Wallen, Laura Spray

Some of the anecdotal illustrations in this book are true to life and are included with the permission of the persons involved. All other illustrations are composites of real situations, and any resemblance to people living or dead is coincidental.

Some of this material appeared in different form in *Baylor Magazine* and *The Langford Review*.

Unless otherwise identified, all Scripture quotations in this publication are taken from the *New Revised Standard Version* (NRSV), copyright © 1989, by the Division of Christian Education of the National Council of the Churches of Christ in the USA, used by permission, all rights reserved. Other versions used include: the *American Standard Version* (ASV) and the *King James Version* (KJV).

Published in association with Jill Grosjean at Jill Grosjean Literary Agency, Sag Harbor, NY, jill6981@ aol.com.

Library of Congress Cataloging-in-Publication Data

Garrett, Greg.
   Crossing myself : a story of spiritual rebirth / Greg Garrett.
      p. cm.
   ISBN 1-57683-856-0
   1. Garrett, Greg. 2. Christian biography. 3. Spiritual healing. 4. Depression, Mental.
   5. Depression, Mental--Religious aspects--Christianity. I. Title.
   BR1725.G375A3 2006
   283.092--dc22

                              2006009592

Printed in the United States of America

1 2 3 4 5 6 / 10 09 08 07 06

Dios escribe derecho con lineas torcidas.
(God writes straight with crooked lines.)

Old Spanish saying

This book is for the Rev. Dr. Greg Rickel and the people of St. James Episcopal Church, Austin, Texas, who saved me, not just for the next life, but for this one.

CONTENTS

Midway through this journey we call life,
I came to myself in a dark forest
Where I had stepped aside from the right path.

Oh, it hurts to say what this forest seemed,
So wild, rough, and difficult that
Thinking of it, I feel the fear all over again.

So bitter it was that death is hardly more frightening.
But to tell you of the good I found there,
I will tell you of all the things I experienced.

Dante Alighieri
The Inferno

prologue

A woman asked me at lunch today—not in a confronta-
tional way, but just in the I'm-confused way in which it
often comes—"And why are you going to seminary?"

It's a good question, and I get it a lot, and yet I never know
exactly how to answer it, because there's a polite answer and
then there's a real answer. I'm beginning my second year at
the Episcopal Theological Seminary of the Southwest in my
hometown of Austin, Texas, and some people think my being
in seminary is the greatest thing since sliced whatever, and
some people wonder why anyone anywhere would ever want to
become a duly-licensed representative of any sort of organized
religion, especially Christianity.

I looked at this woman. She seemed puzzled, but she had a
kind face and she seemed serious and spiritual and thus unlikely
to laugh at me.

I took a deep breath.

"Five years ago," I said, "I didn't really expect to be alive
today."

There's always an uncomfortable pause here, and I made it
a short one by quickly speaking into the silence. "I really think
of my life now as a gift. That it doesn't belong to me anymore.

And so I want to give it serving other people. And that's what I'm learning to do in seminary."

She nodded, slowly, and told me some things about her own life, and the world started revolving again.

I don't think of my story as my own anymore either, because I know that so many other people will recognize themselves or someone they love in it. So I want to give it to serve other people too, and that's what you'll find in the pages that follow.

Mostly this book follows my life from the year 2000, when my chronic depression and insomnia became dangerous, to my lunch, earlier today, in August of 2005, and it tells a story about brokenness becoming wholeness, fear becoming faith, and despair turning to hope.

We're going to pass through some dark places along the way, some weary years, and it may be a help to you in the dark times I talk about to know that there is hope, there is love, that things do get better.

I'm living proof.

So if you feel hurt or alone or out of control, if you feel broken or scared, if you're wondering why you're still alive when your heart is shattered in your chest, or if you know someone who fits this description, then you're especially welcome here.

This book is for you.

Turn the page, and I'll tell you a story about how God brought me out of darkness and into the light.

UNCTION

last rites

Five years ago, in the summer of 2000, after I'd had another gut-wrenching argument with my wife, I found myself standing on a traffic island at the intersection of St. Francis and West Manhattan in Santa Fe, New Mexico. I was looking away to the north, because St. Francis is also the route of US 285 through Santa Fe, and I was hoping a heavily-loaded semi might come into town and hit the lights just exactly right.

Here's what I meant that afternoon by "exactly right": A truck that managed to miss all the red lights coming into town might be going a good 45 or 50 mph when it reached me, and if I stepped into the road in front of it, there was a pretty good chance I would get squashed like a bug.

In the summer of 2004, the man I am now drove to that intersection, turned left down Manhattan toward the house where my family and I lived that awful summer, and I saw that there is an adobe-walled church, Westminster Presbyterian, right there at the corner where I almost took my life.

When I saw it, I remembered how I had passed the church on that afternoon, weeping so hard that I was weaving like a drunk down the middle of the street.

And seeing the church also reminded me that I had stopped there when I saw a large sign that said "Peace," which is what I lacked more than anything, and that I laughed, hard, although it was not a sound you would have wanted to hear.

Then I stood in the street and spoke a challenge for God as I prepared to move past it on that dark afternoon: "You can't help me. And you can't stop me."

I was so confident in my own ability to decide at least this much of my fate, so secure in my lack of faith, that it was only very recently that I understood the truth: that God had both stopped me — and saved me.

How that happened, how I was transformed into a person who not only can't imagine trying to step in front of a speeding vehicle but has become someone who wants to try to save other people — well, that is the story I have to tell, and although, like many stories, it could go back to my birth — or before it — I want to start it five years ago, in that dreadful year of 2000.

It was in 2000 that I first started thinking seriously about killing myself.

By "thinking," I don't mean the idle sort of speculation we do sometimes when we are feeling sorry for ourselves in a maudlin moment: Oh, woe is me, better that I had never been born. And I don't mean the adolescent vision of weeping mourners who would see how much they missed me: Oh, don't they wish they'd treated me nicer when I was around.

No, what I mean is that in the winter and spring of 2000, I started thinking seriously about just exactly how I could cause myself to die.

I had suffered from chronic serious depression for many years, since long before I knew what it was called, in fact. Since my adolescence I had accustomed myself to the idea that the ways of this life were stale, weary, and unprofitable. Even though I had two sons I loved beyond reason, even though I had tenure at a fine university and that summer I finished what would be my first published novel, I couldn't see much of a point to life.

Actually, for a good fifteen years I hadn't much cared if I lived or died. There was, in fact, a certain freedom to that, to seeing that when the plane started to buck like a bronco I was the only one who didn't freak, to knowing I could gladly run into a burning house to try to save someone because I didn't care about the consequences. So I had been perfectly content to die, if it happened. But it was in 2000 that my serotonin-starved brain, my nightly insomnia, my dissolving marriage, my overwhelming guilt, and my feeble faith sat down, took a meeting, and came to this conclusion:

It would be better to be dead, maybe even right now, than to go on living like this.

You have probably heard that suicide is a cry for help, and maybe, sometimes, with some people, that might be true. It's more true with fumbling attempts, of course — the person who expects to be caught, the person who leaves clues or doors open. I'll grant that those people are dramatically announcing something to somebody. But people who have actually decided to step off are doing something else entirely, something that people who have never suffered from Big D Depression can scarcely fathom. They've reached one or more of the same decisions that I reached that year: that life was too painful, that I was unworthy to live, that there was no hope.

As I walked down the street in Santa Fe that afternoon, you may be sure I wasn't crying for help. I was crying because I believed that death was my best option, and you may also be sure that this is a pretty horrible thing to feel.

Ah, but what kind of death? Suicide is a tricky thing, especially if you're genetically encoded to be a responsible person. I knew that I would have to die in such a way that my wife, Tinamarie, and my boys, Jake and Chandler, would still get my life insurance, and I looked over my policy carefully before I discovered the good news. After a lengthy break-in period — to discourage those opportunistic suiciders, I guess — I could kill myself pretty much any old way and my family could still live happily ever after.

That was also good news because, frankly, a lot of the less obvious ways I had been thinking about seemed less than foolproof. For example, earlier in 2000, after one particularly virulent early-morning argument with Tinamarie in front of our horrified son Chandler — all of our arguments were in front of Chandler when we were married, and most after — I had taken the car out onto Interstate 35, which is the major north-south artery in Texas, gotten up to about 85, and scoped out the bridge abutment I'd rammed some characters into in one of my novels.

In *Cycling* I killed them dead as dead, but in real life, I thought there were too many variables. Sure, I could be going fast, it was unyielding concrete, but what if I lived? Then I'd be disabled and depressed, and probably unable to ever control my own fate again. What if, as a result of the crash, I lost those few things that made life tolerable and couldn't do anything about it? Now that would be hell.

No, the best solution was a handgun. They're expressly designed to kill people, and on the afternoon that Tinamarie and I had argued in Santa Fe, I had actually gone down to the basement and torn through the closets of the house we were sitting, hoping to discover the heavy cold steel of a Smith & Wesson in some box way up high.

If I'd found one, I would have shot myself. Right then. Right there. I was ready to die at that moment, and the fact that the people who owned the house were pacifist granola people like ourselves was the first gift God provided. In those first moments when I was so emotionally overwhelmed that I would definitely have stepped into any abyss, there was no conveniently located one to be found.

That's what sent me out the door and down the street, what had me talking to God as I approached the intersection. You might be wondering why I had taken the time to talk to God on my way to death; we don't traditionally associate belief in God with such despair. And let's get this straight: I did believe in God. I was raised in the church. I had had a so-called conversion experience when I was a kid. Immediately before we had come to Santa Fe, I had even taught Sunday school, assisted with baptism, and occasionally sung in the choir of a church whose members loved me and cared about me.

So I had some sense at the back of my raging brain that what I wanted to do was not okay with the universe. But I had also had some bad experiences with God—or rather, let's say, with God's posse—and although it's true that I had been a guest in God's house from time to time, we were not exactly close. I still received the occasional e-mail — a burst of sunlight through dark clouds, or the kind of revelation of grace through literature, music, or movies that Walker Percy described as "a message in a bottle." But we were like e-mail pals who never do a face-to-face, or, rather, I was like one of those people who sits at the receiving end of a one-sided correspondence, glances at the message, and never responds. Eventually the other person seems to stop sending, and if you are as dense as I am, you may even wonder why.

But more likely, if you're like me, you get so caught up in the white noise of life that you never even notice the silence.

That I stopped and talked to God for a moment on my way to death is not, then, unaccountable. People have always wanted to make their peace, get something off their chests, or state their case. In Catholic traditions, there is a ceremony commonly called "last rites," or sometimes "extreme unction." For Catholics, it's a sacramental sending off, one last chance to make things right with God before you step off into the unknown. For me, that moment of stopping in the middle of Manhattan was my last remembrance that there was a God — and my final rejection of any comfort that God had to offer.

It seemed to me that God hadn't been much help to me in my unhappy life, off at some distant workstation. And so my final message to God might have been one of rejection, me talking back to a computer screen. I can't help but shake my head in rueful amusement when I realize that I might have died without ever knowing that if I'd so much as put the tips of my fingers to the keyboard to e-mail God back, I would have found a message from God saying, let's go have coffee.

You know that I'm writing these words, so obviously I didn't die that day in Santa Fe. And I didn't die after Tinamarie left me, when I counted up my sleeping pills and thought about taking them all, and I didn't die the following fall when I called up my best friend, Chris, after I'd caused a drunken scene at Tinamarie's birthday party and told him I felt like I was about to do something bad to myself.

I didn't die any of those times. But I came very close, and especially so on that afternoon.

I can't tell you how long I stood out there on the median on that day—it could have been a minute, it could have been ten. The thoughts and images were flashing through my brain like it was a Cray superprocessor. And I can't tell you what I must have looked like to people driving by, although I can imagine—a grown man, weeping so hard that he's bent almost double, watching the road to the north with a desperate expression on his face.

But I can tell you now why I didn't do it, and it doesn't have to do with any of the rational reasons that flashed through my head. I didn't care that it would leave my sons bereft and desolate; I thought they were better off without a father like me. I didn't care what my parents would think—even though they had just left earlier that day after an extended visit—or what my colleagues would think, or what kind of message this would be to the students who loved me. When you're in agony, none of that matters.

I didn't do it because in that last moment the power of empathy God gave me to write with put me in the heads of the two people who would be most directly affected by my wish to die. I imagined how Tinamarie would feel when she got the news, how she would blame herself, how it would break her. And crazy as I might have been, cruel as I might have been, I was never petty, and I never stopped loving her. I couldn't do that.

And I also imagined the poor truck driver, his trailer heavy with tall pine trees from the Sangre de Cristos, so heavy that he'd have no chance at all to stop if some complete idiot stepped off the curb in front of him. I could imagine the brakes squealing. I could hear the thump. I could imagine what it would feel like to know that I had rolled over somebody, run him down without meaning to, certainly, but all the same he would be dead as yesterday's news, and I would remember that every time I climbed up into the cab to do my job.

I stood there for a long time.

I was ready and willing to die.

But I didn't want to hurt anybody else in the doing of it.

And so, finally, after two minutes, or ten, however long it was, I walked back across St. Francis and down Manhattan, in the direction of my house. I was still sobbing, and this may be the saddest thing of all: I was bereft because I really wanted to die and saw now that I could not. At that moment, as paradoxical as it seems, it seemed like my only hope was passing out of my hands.

That I didn't die that day was a blessing, for me, perhaps for others. That, at least, is my hope. And the reasons I didn't step off may have seemed purely personal, but I can see now that they were also spiritual. Although I tried to make God sit this dance out, clearly, as Jules says in *Pulp Fiction*, "God got involved." Although I didn't yet understand it, I had been saved for something.

In the summer of 2001, I began attending a multicultural Episcopal church in Austin, Texas, which is where Tinamarie, Chandler, and I landed after we left Santa Fe in August of 2000. Tinamarie and I split up shortly after we arrived in Austin, and the first two years there were the worst of my life. Much of my understanding about how and why I survived has come from my contact with the people of St. James parish, with the rector, Greg Rickel, and with the Anglican way of seeing the world as charged with the glory of God. This sacramental vision is at the heart of all I believe now; it has finally helped me make some sense out of those unaccountable e-mails from God, helped me see how God might make something straight out of all the crooked paths I've trudged.

We believe that the sacraments are signs of God's grace moving in the world, what the *Book of Common Prayer* calls "outward and visible signs of inward and spiritual grace." Protestants and Catholics disagree on exactly what the sacraments are or how many — most low-church traditions (I grew up a Southern Baptist, and my family has Assembly of God and Methodist roots, so low church is my heritage) say there are only two, baptism and marriage; Catholic, Orthodox, and the Anglican/Episcopalian traditions typically say there are seven formal sacraments (baptism, confirmation, confession, communion, marriage, ordination, and unction). But however many there are, and whether they are formal or informal, sacraments are things of the greatest power.

I can tell you from experience — they can save your life.

Frank Griswold, the presiding bishop of the Episcopal Church, explained the power of sacraments in this way:

In Hebrew, "word" carries with it notions of occurrence as well as speech. Words therefore happen; they take place. The sacraments and sacramental rites are therefore enacted words whose force and power once again derive from the risen One. "You have revealed yourself to me, O Christ, face to face. I have met you in your sacraments." These bold words of St. Ambrose underscore the formative and developmental effect of our sacramental participation in season and out of season, and at the different turnings of our lives.[1]

In season and out of season, in joy and in weeping, sacraments can give us a tangible connection to God, can create pathways for God to speak to us, can help us believe that God is really there.

I know all this because the sacraments are how God convinced me that there was a life worth living. It was through the sacraments that God at last turned my grief and despair into joy, at last brought me into communion with him and with other people seeking him. If I had only understood then the sacrament we Episcopalians call "unction," which involves a priest's anointing the afflicted with oil, I would have understood that I wasn't alone, that, in fact, I was never — and will never be — alone.

Greg, my rector, tells me that the oil for unction is blessed every year by the bishop at a ceremony where the priests reaffirm their ordination vows. "Then," he says, "the oil is blessed, put in vials, and sent out with the priests to be used throughout the year. The oil placed on the head of those being baptized or in unction is an outward sign of their connection at that moment to the greater Church, the Body of Christ. In a sense, the Church is there, as God is there."

I didn't believe that then; I know better now.

So the story I have to tell you is a sacramental one, and if I write it well, it too will be made up of words with power behind them. It too will be lined with grace. And in its simplest outline, it will be like that simple story Jesus told about the prodigal son: I was dead, and now I live; I was lost, and now am found.

I was blind, and now I begin, at last, to see.

prayers for the departed

Everyone I know goes away in the end.

TRENT REZNOR, "HURT"

What does it mean to say that I was dead, and now I live? For surely that is what has happened to me five years on, although getting to the story of my joyful life in 2005 requires that we first walk through the valley of the shadow.

Just about every day last summer, after I moved into my garage apartment at the Episcopal Theological Seminary of the Southwest in July of 2004, I rode my bike the three miles or so from the seminary down to the hike and bike trail that does a long lazy loop around Town Lake and also, more importantly, takes me to Barton Springs. This trail along the impounded Colorado River is the sweaty heart of Austin; here the hip and the homeless, the young and the not-so-young, the terminally tattooed and those of virginal skin, the dog people and the cat people and the snake people mingle, jogging, walking, biking, or propelling wheelchairs.

If the Town Lake trail is the heart of the city, then Barton Springs is the soul. This spring-fed pool is how Austinites measure the environmental health of the city. If we have a screed, it is not "What would Jesus do?" It is "What would this do to the Springs?" It is one of the first places tourists visit, and on an average afternoon I might hear German, French, and Japanese spoken around me. I come to the Springs to write; so does my rector, Greg, who works on his sermons here every Monday afternoon. Barton Springs is also, incidentally, a place to swim — there are all these people in swimsuits hanging about — but I rarely go to swim. Instead I typically climb sweating off my bike and clamber into the cold flowing water that flows over the dam, which captures the Springs for swimming, the water that soon joins the river. Then I sit down at the picnic tables overlooking the Springs, take out my books, or take out my journal and see what it is that I have to say.

Along the way, I pedal past a larger-than-life bronze statue of Stevie Ray Vaughn, the great blues guitarist, and a half mile farther on, in the shade of overgrowing oaks and pecans, a granite bench given by members of some family to remember someone named Chris.

Whenever I pass these reminders of the dead, the gravel chips of the path crunching beneath my tires, I cross myself and say a prayer. At first I felt a little self-conscious, but now I have given myself over to it entirely and almost do it without thinking.

Same with the impromptu memorial on the pier of the railroad bridge over South Lamar — the flowers, the painted message remembering a boy named Garth,

Fair-sailing boy

Don't drink and drive
You might kill someone's kid.

When I pass Garth's monument, I also cross myself and breathe a prayer. It is part of what I do in church now, every Sunday, and like faith is supposed to do, it has become part of my everyday.

There are six forms of the Prayers of the People in the *Book of Common Prayer*, and all of them ask prayers for the departed. Perhaps the best known and most poetic is this:

> Give to the departed eternal rest.
> Let light perpetual shine upon them.

We never remembered the dead in the Baptist tradition; we prayed for the families, which we also do at St. James. But clearly in the Episcopal tradition, something different was going on, something, I suspected, Catholic and idolatrous.

When I asked Greg why it was we prayed for the dead, it was out of real curiosity and with some real skepticism. From my experience, death was the end of pain, the end of suffering, something to be welcomed, not something to be feared. Even if death was nothingness, obliteration, there had been plenty of days when that sounded better than what I had going. And frankly, those lines — "eternal rest" and "light perpetual" — sound like a consummation devoutly to be wished. Cake with icing. So why do the dead need our prayers?

"Well," Greg began his e-mail,

> we pray for the departed because we think their essence is changed, not obliterated. Death is not final — that is the Christian belief. Our prayers for them make this a living reality in our lives together in this part of the Kingdom. Our prayers for

the departed say again that we believe in the Cloud of Witnesses of which they are now a part, praying with us, in their new part of the Kingdom.

I wrestled a long time with this idea, with life after death, with all this heaven stuff.

Because frankly, I don't think the carrot and stick of the afterlife should have an effect on the faith we choose, or on our moral behavior in this life. When I became a Christian as a young person, it was because my pastor in Oklahoma had scared me witless about dying in my sin and going to hell. I became a Christian not because I really understood the gospel message, or particularly wanted to be a good person. I just didn't want to go to hell and burn forever.

That would suck.

So why would someone who struggles with the idea of a hereafter pray for the dead? Well, that's what I've been wrestling with. It's not to reposition the dead from one place to another, Purgatory to Heaven, for example — Episcopalians don't believe that. We're not even praying for our loved ones to have a better seat at the table. But I can tell you one reason why it has been important for me to pray when I pass Stevie Ray Vaughn's statue, whenever I see any memorial left for someone who has died. When I see them, I remember that it represents someone who was loved and is now gone, that the monument represents a family that is no longer complete. That there was — and may still be — sadness to heal, brokenness to complete.

Stevie Ray has been dead for over a decade, and I think it would be fair to say that I miss him almost every day, even though I never met the man. Much much more would those who knew and loved him — or who knew Garth, the fair-sailing boy who I know only from his painted name on a bridge. I know this.

My Grandpa Chuck, my mom's father, died almost twenty years ago, and yet there isn't a week when he doesn't come to my mind. I feel his absence like a hole in my heart. As I type these words, there are tears in my eyes.

Multiply that pain by a million monuments, by a million grieving families and communities of friends, and there is so much agony in the world that I can scarcely fathom it.

It makes me glad that I didn't add to that reservoir of pain and loss of my own accord.

Although I rarely think of this anymore, there could have been one of those monuments to me somewhere — a tasteful plaque at Baylor University, where I teach, maybe a tree planted in my memory, or maybe a cross and some plastic flowers at that intersection in Santa Fe. I know and feel what I could not let myself know and feel five years ago: that I matter. If something were to happen to me, I would be mourned.

I did not die then, thank God, but it has become clearer and clearer that there has been some kind of terminal change involved in my progress from despair to joy, from the guy who wanted to kill himself in Santa Fe five years ago to the one who started seminary last fall.

In a very real sense, I think you could say that the me who wanted to die did die. Not the way he planned, perhaps even hoped. But he's dead all the same, and I hope he rests in peace.

The apostle Paul says in the sixth chapter of the letter to the Romans that someone who dies with Christ in baptism rises like Christ into new life. The old me who looked at the world with despair, fear, and resentment is dead and gone. He hasn't shown his face for two years, and I don't expect him back — ever.

The biggest part of that resurrection was my coming into the body of Christ — becoming a person of living faith, becoming a part of the community of St. James Episcopal. There were other parts — little flashes of grace that came through my writing or through therapy, from time spent alone and time spent with those who love me.

And it wasn't, as you will see, instant. I stumbled through my days for a long time even after I accepted that I had no power over my life and no hope without God. The first few months I was at St. James, I sat trembling in my pew, sometimes literally, and not just because the air conditioning is always on too high.

But messages kept coming over the line the whole time I was sick and over the time I was getting better, and those messages told me, *Don't give up hope. You were made for something better.*

I think messages from God may come in a lot of ways. I'm open now to the idea that the letter to the Romans may speak to me, or that a beautifully written e-mail may change my life. I also think it's possible that I may find insight in a billboard I streak past at eighty miles an hour, or that I may hear the voice of God in an idle line of conversation or in a line from a song by Coldplay. That's what the sacramental vision of the world means to me: If God is in the world, then God can be glimpsed everywhere, if I am only open to the possibility.

Last summer, as I began to think over the past years and how to tell this story, I ran across something in the local alternative newspaper, the *Austin Chronicle*: Every five years or so, our body has shed and regenerated every one of the cells that makes up our person, so we literally are not the same persons we were five years ago. Not a single cell remains of our old selves. "You have reincarnated, without having to endure the inconvenience of dying."[1]

Well, my death would have been more than inconvenient to my sons, of course, and to those who loved me and wanted to help me.

It would have been tragic.

That is why I pray for those left behind, because of that pain, that sadness. But Greg's words spark thoughts in me, as they often do. When I was a person of no hope — when in fact the oblivion of death was the best thing I could conjure up for myself — then thinking about the survivors was also the only compassionate response, the only way prayer could have relevance.

But now that I have become a person of great hope, a person again willing to believe in things I can't see, I've been given another reason to pray.

I don't know — objectively — if my prayers for the departed make any difference in the cosmic scheme of things. God doesn't need my urging to gather in those who have died in the hope of life eternal.

But those prayers make a difference in me.

My favorite of the prayers for the departed is a prayer for "all who have died in the communion of your Church, and those whose faith is known to you alone, that with all the saints, they may have rest in that place where there is no pain or grief, but life eternal, we pray to you, O Lord."

Pain and grief have been formative emotions for me; I have felt them, and now I want to help others as they wrestle with them. In this new life I've been given, I want to live with joy and purpose. That is the purpose of everything that follows.

And if there is a cloud of witnesses, if death is really only, as Anne Lamott says, just a big change of address, if I really could be in that number when the saints go marching in?

Well, then, that would be cake with icing.

And I do love cake with icing.

CONFESSION

family history

There is a crack in everything.
That's how the light gets in.

LEONARD COHEN, "ANTHEM"

I have a picture of my Grandpa Chuck, my mother's father, on a bookshelf in the tiny apartment where I live now at the Episcopal Seminary of the Southwest. He's wearing a straw cowboy hat — a work hat, not a dress hat — and he has a sort of sidelong smile on his face. The baby he's propping on the hood of a car is me, yet, strangely, the hands, the arms that are holding me gently in place are mine, the very ones I see as I look down at the computer keyboard.

While I don't own a cowboy hat, in some ways, we are that alike.

The baby me in the picture is now the same age as the grandfather in the picture, and as I look at the two of us, I remember a salient fact: Depression is hereditary. My mother had it; my older son has it. My grandfather's brothers fought it, faltered, drank themselves to death. And when I look at the eyes of my granddad in this picture, as in other pictures, I feel pretty certain that there are oceans of sadness there.

I'll never know for certain: My grandpa died twenty years ago, shortly after he had the chance to hold my older son, Jake, in those same arms — another picture I have. Twenty years. After all this time, writing about him now clenches my stomach with grief.

I've always felt that Chuck was the relative I most resembled — and most wanted to resemble. I admired my father's musical talent and easy way with people, my mother's faith and devotion, but I always thought — still do — that my grandpa hung the sun and moon. A farmer and rancher in Western Oklahoma, he brought wheat and alfalfa up from the red sandy dirt, steered a string of pickup trucks bouncing along worn ruts through his pastures in search of straying cattle, and taught me much of what I know about being a man.

We have more than the same arms; we have the same ears, the same frame, the same quiet and shy disposition. He was simultaneously the strongest and gentlest man I have ever known; in another of my favorite pictures, Chuck has kittens crawling over and on his hands, those hands hardened by decades of building fences and hauling hay. My mom and my grandma Rose agree that they only saw Chuck angry once in their lives, when a cow he was dosing with medicine stepped on his hand. It's interesting — he almost brained that cow with a hammer before he got control of himself, stepped back, probably whistled a tuneless tune under his breath.

I know a little bit about how that kind of ridiculous and out of proportion rage can come bubbling up unexpectedly out of such a quiet pool. It's a sign that there's a deep anger or unhappiness that can't find an outlet in everyday life, and it makes me feel even more kinship with my granddad. There was more going on deep inside him than he ever let on or let out. I imagine that, like me, he had hard nights and gray days, and on that occasion, at least, he was pushed over the edge by the cosmic unfairness of things. My friends at the seminary say I have the composure and compassion of the Buddha, but they also say they'd never want to see me mad, and Tinamarie could tell them that they're absolutely right.

Chuck never, to my remembrance, told any of his grandchildren that he loved them — such things were not done in his generation in any case — but the rough affection with which he treated us, the teasing and name-calling, tells me worlds now. "All right, you skunks," he used to say to my brother Jeff and me, "let's go to town." He'd take us to get our hair cut — short and bristly, like his crew cut — then off to the Hi-De-Ho, what passed for a restaurant in the small town of Watonga in the days before franchising. He was showing us off, although I didn't realize it then, claiming us as his own.

I regretted for years that he'd never told us of the love I felt sure he had for us. Then when I first saw *The Princess Bride*, which is now a favorite and much-memorized movie in my family, I finally understood. The crusty and crotchety old grandfather played by Peter Falk, who narrates the story of Westley the farm boy and his great love, Buttercup, tells us early in the film that whenever Westley responds to Buttercup's demands by saying, "As you wish," what he's really saying is "I love you." When, at movie's end, the grandson asks his grandfather to come back the next day and read him the story again and the grandfather replies, "As you wish," a lightbulb went off over my head that explained many things, most especially the love of the quiet man in the picture on my bookshelf who would never let me fall.

We are the sum of our histories, our genes, and our chemicals, and nowhere is this more true than with a disease like depression. I was raised by good people who loved me in a religion that was bad for me and a culture that was poisonous for creative and sensitive people; I inherited genes for musical talent, faithfulness, a love of words and of the outdoors, and a bad case of chronic depression; then when I was in my late teens, some fateful chemical change took place inside my brain affecting the serotonin I needed to regulate my moods, triggered perhaps by hormones, perhaps by diet, perhaps by listening to Ozzy Osbourne and Van Halen at high volumes.

Okay, I'm kidding about that last thing. Really.

But those other pieces of my history intersected, and I can remember a pall of gray falling over my life even in my teen years. It was a light cloak compared to the gray that would come. Girls, beer, music, and good times with friends could still pull me out of it and make me feel better. Joy was not an alien concept.

But it was there. I could tell that I saw the world differently from many of my friends, that I was infected with a negativity, a hopelessness that was remarkable in someone who had walked on the planet for so little time. I was also victimized by insomnia, but in those days I was young, strong, and it seemed more like a romantic badge of honor than something that could cause me problems. It gave me more time to party. I worked late shifts. I threw a paper route in the dead of night. I encouraged girls to sneak out of their houses and into my car at three in the morning.

Then one gray day in my early twenties, married to my high school sweetheart and with a long and presumably productive life ahead of me, I remember thinking to myself as I drove to college, *I wish I were dead.*

This wasn't prompted by a disagreement, by a betrayal, by abandonment or physical pain. It was just that, all of a sudden, I couldn't see any real reason to be alive.

That was the first time my depression encouraged me to compare life and death and to decide that there might be more to be hoped for on the death side of the ledger.

The first time, but hardly the last.

One ongoing factor was that my personal life was and continued to be a mess. My first marriage ended badly, and my second was filled with pain and distance, and although I was becoming professionally successful, a much-admired professor and a publishing writer, throughout my twenties and into my early thirties, depression colored my thoughts. One day, on my way back from a research trip to Washington DC, my plane hit serious turbulence and suddenly began to dip, buck, and shake like a mechanical bronco in a Houston honky-tonk. People screamed, peanuts and drinks flew every which way, and the flight attendants had fear in their eyes while their lips encouraged everyone to stay calm.

In fact, I was calm.

I wasn't the least bit afraid. That's what I remembered most when we landed, as I was driving back home. I later used this situation as the beginning scene of a novel, in fact, because it seemed to be a pretty dramatic one. What does it mean when everyone around you is hysterical that you're all going to die in flaming wreckage and you could care less?

When actually, you're sort of rooting for it?

The final stage in this growth of my depression came with the birth of my son Chandler in October of 1997. By now I was married to Tinamarie, my third wife (Third! Tell me anyone grows up saying, "When I marry my third wife — "), and many things about that felt good. I was reaching some sort of accommodation with organized religion after many years of fleeing from it. At that time, Tinamarie was a devout evangelical Christian, so I was willing to be fairly active in a moderate Baptist church where many of my friends from Baylor University were members. While I wasn't moved by the style of worship and actually didn't feel much connection with God anywhere except in nature, it was good to have some kind of community.

When we went off to Oregon on sabbatical and Tinamarie got pregnant, I did feel cut off and a little apprehensive, but I loved being in the mountains, riding my bike daily, cross-country skiing, camping along the Rogue River. When we came back to Texas, I was sure that everything would be okay.

Only, when Chandler was born, my insomnia went from bad to impossible. Between his almost hourly waking and early morning rising, many nights I didn't sleep at all; I felt lucky to get some sleep every three or four days. Sometimes I'd get less than a dozen hours of sleep in a week's time.

It made me crazy.

I wish there were some other way to put it. Here's a place in this story where I'd love to mince words, to say this in a way that makes me look better, saner, kinder. But the fact of the matter is, after Chandler was born, I became a mean, angry, and desperate person. Not every moment of every day, I'll grant. But more often than I want to tell, things bubbled up from that calm pool that seemed to be me, things that I'm ashamed to own, yet honesty demands that I name them and claim them.

It made me crazy.

I don't know if the depression affected the insomnia, or vice versa. All I know is that the two of them together were a lethal combination. I was so tired I had little control over my emotions, and so hopeless that I didn't care to control them. They were so close to the surface now that when Tinamarie and I fought, which we did more and more often, I could fling anger like monkeys toss excrement. I watched from some strange clinical distance as I screamed at the woman I loved, as our toddler hid behind her in fear. I felt out of control of my life, of my marriage, of my self.

Although I never struck Tinamarie or Chandler, I began to write short stories about abusive fathers; my emotional life has always found its way into my pages, and through the filter of my art, I saw clearly that what I was doing was abusive, was scarring my family. I wrote a story about an abusive husband who thrusts his hands into scalding water to punish himself. I began that story with an epigraph from the Psalms: "My sin is ever before me."

And so it was. I managed to muddle through my days, to teach well, to do some writing. I've always been a private person who hid behind walls. You would have had to look closely to see that I was falling apart and taking my family with me. I was still, as mental health professionals describe it, "functional," but not by much.

Late at night, tossing and turning in another part of the house from my family, I began to consider that unless I could get help, maybe it would be better if I were dead. Maybe it was already too late — maybe the damage I was doing to my wife, to my son, would never be healed.

After they had gone to bed, I used to sit at my desk, awake, my stomach tight with self-loathing and remorse, and try to understand my life by turning it into thinly disguised fiction.

I began to think about getting in a car and disappearing someplace where I couldn't hurt anyone anymore, where no one could hurt me.

I also began to think about getting into a car and ramming it into a bridge abutment at high speed.

I was a messy stew of need, guilt, remorse, desire, loneliness, and hopelessness, and yet I was surprised to find that Tinamarie didn't want to be around me. We bought a beautiful old home and moved into it with Chandler. We hoped for a new beginning. But the hits kept coming, and then one night in early 2000 Tinamarie was so late coming back from a friend's house — and who could blame her? I wouldn't want to come home to me either — that I feared something had happened, and when she did get in, we had our biggest fight to date, epic and vicious.

At last, I snatched the car keys from her and drove out toward I-35, where I knew from my use of it in my novel *Cycling* that there was a conveniently-situated bridge abutment.

On reflection, I can see that my thinking that night on doing myself in was split — maybe 35 percent of me was willing to do it, maybe forty. It wasn't like the 50 percent or greater urging that I later felt on that afternoon in Santa Fe. But it was a consideration, a definite option.

I gave it serious thought.

And at last, I slowed down to seventy, passed the bridge

abutment by, drove country roads for hours until finally I parked the car and sat.

Tinamarie had encouraged me to go to counseling. I had told her I would. But although I'd asked some questions, located someone I thought I might get on with, I had not actually pulled the trigger. I was like Anne Lamott, who in her essay "Hunger" writes of going to a specialist on eating disorders and telling her that she's not ready to do what she has to do to get better, but that she's "getting ready to be ready."[1]

That's about where I was: I was thinking about thinking about getting ready to be ready.

And now, as I thought about it, I realized that if things continued this way much longer I was going to lose my wife. I was going to lose my son. The good things about my life were going to vanish, and I was going to be left alone with nothing but the darkness. And while Tinamarie wasn't blameless in our troubles — none of us ever is — I bore the onus. If I couldn't get better, then life as I knew it was over, even if I could somehow go on living.

I've wondered, sometimes, if my granddad suffered as I have suffered, and if he did, if he had a friend to talk to, if he had a faith that helped him make sense of things, if sitting by the pond on a sunny day or working in the outdoors somehow gave him the strength to go on. But still, I imagine him sometimes sitting in the cab of his truck and looking at the far horizon and feeling totally lost and alone.

Then I imagine him heading off to do his work, feeding his cows, plowing his fields, taking my grandma to the Methodist church in Watonga on Sundays, sitting around in the early morning with other farmers over coffee. Sometimes the everyday heroism of people just amazes me. Who knows what the person sitting next to us on the plane is wrestling with, how much effort it takes the man in the pulpit, the woman at the podium, the kid behind the cash register, just to walk through their days?

Well, okay. I know. And I want to honor them — and the people who help them, and the God who loves them.

My Grandpa Chuck was a farmer and a rancher, a father and grandfather, and I loved and love him beyond reason; he is my hero.

He never, to my knowledge, wrote a book, song, or essay, but he was, like me, a lover of stories, and that love was most strongly satisfied by reading every thin western ever written by Louis L'Amour. In each of those stories, a cowboy faced a menace, failed miserably and was beaten within an inch of his life, crawled away to recover, a long and tenuous process, and returned at last to fight his way to victory.

Grandpa used to say that Louis L'Amour's books were so much alike that he could go back and read them every year or two and forget that he'd ever seen them before. What I think now is that they were all just one story, told over and over again, as are all the great stories that we need to hear. Those stories reminded him — and remind me — that life is difficult. That it can beat us until we're bloody, until we need to drag ourselves into a cave in a lava flow or an abandoned line shack or into the arms of a caring healer if there's to be any chance of our survival.

Suffering is a part of every story. But so is the chance of completing the circle, of coming back to life, of winning the day.

The Rite II burial service in the *Book of Common Prayer* contains this prayer:

Grant, O Lord, to all who are bereaved the spirit of faith and courage, that they may have strength to meet the days to come with steadfastness and patience; not sorrowing as those without hope, but in thankful remembrance of your great goodness, and in the joyful expectation of eternal life with those they love.

I believe in burials, because I have witnessed them, because I have been myself buried alive.

But if we survive — if we don't bleed to death in the dust of an unnamed desert or freeze under the black skies of the high plains or run our cars into unyielding concrete — then there is hope. Even if we can't see it. Maybe especially if we can't see it.

My Grandpa Chuck lived a life that showed me how to be strong and kind, to give to others, and to persevere. He represented the face of a kind and gentle God for me in a time when all I had heard preached was an angry and frightening one. And if all I can do now is proclaim my thanks and tell you his story, maybe that will do, until that joyful expectation can be fulfilled, until the day that the circle is finally complete.

direction

And Solomon said, "The LORD has told us that
he will be present in the deep darkness."

2 CHRONICLES 6:1

I was not a very good patient, or subject, or whatever you call
the person who comes to therapy saying that he or she wants
to change and get better. I can admit that now, could probably
see it even then.

When I started going to see Don in the spring of 2000, I didn't
realize that it was life-or-death work we were doing. I thought
we were talking about self-esteem, exhaustion, rage, and inade-
quacy, all the piddling symptoms of the spiritual cancer that
had metastasized into my heart and brain and bones. Then a
string of crises in my marriage distracted us from the real work
that needed to be done.

And then, all of a sudden, it seemed, I found myself thinking about death all the time.

It wasn't Don's fault. He asked good questions and listened
with compassion to the information that I measured out to
him. He made suggestions that I didn't follow, but should have.

He told me that I was suffering from serious depression, that I was in fact a "classical case." It seemed to him that I manifested seven of the nine major symptoms, and probably had three or four of the six types of depression.

I took more pride in that than I should have, maybe, but I was raised to think that anything worth doing is worth doing well.

At our first meeting, Don asked me what I would change about my life if I could.

My answer was so ridiculous, so shallow, that now I think to myself, *Son, no wonder you almost bit the dust.*

I talked about my low self-image, which I think is not a bad insight to recognize; I've written about it elsewhere in these pages with some understanding that it was important to love myself more than I did, which was not at all.

And I said I wanted to publish a book.

Sigh.

After all the years of teaching my students that it was more important to be a good person than a good writer, of telling them that publishing doesn't make you smarter, prettier, or saner, I told Don that I wanted to publish a book.

I thought it would make me feel better about myself, bring in a little money, and give me the sheen of professional success I still thought I lacked.

I don't have to tell you that publishing a book was not one of the two things I most needed to change about my life.

Given the severity of my depression and its organic basis, Don suggested that I consider taking antidepressants and perhaps a sleep aid. He thought that years of not sleeping was not good for me.

I did at least go to the psychiatrist he recommended, who said I had dysthemia, a low-grade chronic depression, but agreed that medicine would probably do me good—it was his opinion that medicine could do everyone good.

He also felt that not sleeping was not good for me.

I probably don't have to tell you that people with low-grade depression do not stand on street corners waiting for a truck to run them over.

But none of that mattered. In those days, we aspired to be a drug-free, nontraditional-medicine family, and anyway, I hated drugs. My constitution wasn't right to be a medicated person. I was allergic to a lot of things, so I usually had serious side-effects when I took something. And anyway, I was too strong and self-reliant to let some little pill try to save the day.

The difference between a little pill and the chamomile, tryptophan, valerian, and other substances I was ingesting trying to get some sleep seems less important now, but for some reason, it mattered then.

I probably don't have to tell you that nothing I bought over the counter, cooked, drank, or sprinkled over my cereal helped me sleep or made me sane.

In that first meeting when he was trying to make a diagnosis, Don had asked me a jarring question, one that made me realize, "Yeah. Okay. That's me."

The question went something like this: "Do you ever feel like you're walking through quicksand?"

And my response was, "Of course. Every minute of every day."

But I think I can refine the experience even further: Serious chronic depression feels like being underwater. Everything is muffled and murky and gray, the light from above is filtered and weakened, and even though you know there's a surface world, you feel you're much more likely to disappear into the deeper darkness below than you are ever to breathe fresh air.

The weight of the world presses in on you. It's hard to breathe.

And sometimes you wonder why you even try to stay afloat.

As I write about it now, two years after my last real experience of depression, I can tell you that even just dipping my toe back into that water is almost unbearable. As Parker Palmer wrote about his own bout with depression, "I still find depression difficult to speak about, because the experience is so unspeakable."[1]

I spent twenty years of my life down there and five of them near the bottom, where there is no light and no air and the pressure can crush you.

I don't want to go back.

But I will, for the sake of all those who are still down there, for those who love them or want to help them, and out of thanks that I was pulled from those depths by a tetherline of grace and faith and community.

Don and I broke off therapy when my family left for Santa Fe in the summer of 2000, and I didn't see anyone during our time up there, and you have seen the results. When I came back to Texas in August, still alive somehow, Don and I resumed our work, and in our first session, I told him most of what had happened: that the summer had been awful, so awful that I started taking the medication I'd been prescribed; that the medication didn't work for me, that it in fact made me more paranoid and psychotic at a time when I was already doing quite well with those things on my own; that my insomnia hadn't cleared up in the mountains as I'd hoped when we left, but had gotten worse; that, after that last horrific fight with Tinamarie, I'd set out to ride the grille of a semi.

I told the story as clearly and calmly as I could, although I choked up more than once; I was still so close to the story that I felt it intensely, and I still wasn't completely sure I'd made the right decision.

Don listened seriously and sadly, and when I was done, he nodded his head gravely and agreed that I'd come as close to killing myself as one can and survive it. Stopping the pain is the most serious reason for suicide, he said, and that had certainly been my reason for wanting to die.

He called it a "watershed event," but it didn't feel shed to me. We returned to it in each of our next meetings, sometimes for a moment, sometimes for the whole hour. Then a few weeks later as we were talking about it, Don said something that seemed nonchalant, but, as is usually the way of such things, it was something that would change my life completely.

"Do you know why God saved you?" Don asked me. We didn't talk this way much, because although Don was a devout Christian, I was wandering in the wilderness, and in those days I had had enough of Godtalk.

This question was different though, whether because of the timing or something else. Did I know why God had saved me? In other words, did you know that there is a God, and that this God does not want you to kill yourself? That this God has plans for you?

I had to shake my head. I had no idea why God, if there was

one, would save me. I think I may have managed to whisper "No." Because, as I mentioned, I was still not so sure that being alive was such a good thing for me. "Why?"

Don leaned over a bit, and the look on his face was earnest. "So you could save someone else."

"Ah," I said. FYI: "Ah" is what I say when I hear you talking but I'm not listening.

I didn't want to believe it then because, as I said, I wasn't so sure I was going to be around to save anyone, and it was pretty clear to me at that moment that if I was, all my attention had to be directed toward trying to at least keep myself from sinking any further.

When we came back from Santa Fe in August, we had sold our lovely home in Waco and moved to Austin. It's a decision that makes lots of sense if you want to live in a place with great music, restaurants, natural food, and natural beauty. If you want to live, period. But it was a disaster for me.

Austin was in the middle of the Tech Boom, and not only couldn't we come within $100,000 of affording a house like we'd sold, the only apartment we could find for immediate move-in was a one bedroom ridiculously out of our price range. Because it was only a one bedroom and there were three of us, Tinamarie had to tell the apartment managers that I didn't really live there, that I'd be living in Waco during the week while I taught and coming home to visit on the weekends.

And you know, that's how it felt — like I didn't really live there — and not just because I had to sneak in and out of my own home. Tinamarie had been coming to Austin for months before we left for Santa Fe, had made a ton of friends, and together they went to parties, went dancing or clubbing, ate out.

I was driving 100 miles each way to teach at Baylor three days a week, and when I was home, I was so exhausted that all I really wanted to do was nothing.

And even if I had wanted to do something, I knew not a soul in Austin and it seemed unlikely that I ever would, because making friends requires a degree of mental health that I did not then possess.

So on those nights when Tinamarie went out, I stayed home with Chandler, and I lay awake until she came home, and then lay awake for hours after she fell asleep, and then another morning came.

In our tiny apartment, with Chandler snoring softly on a pallet next to the bed, I began to have a waking nightmare, began to imagine the walls, the very air closing in on me. I felt a heavy weight settle across my chest and tighten like a tourniquet. For years I've had a daydream or fantasy that comes when I feel like I've lost all control of my life. I imagine that I take a shotgun — one of those impossibly powerful, always-loaded pump shotguns that exist only in movies or video games — and start blasting out the windows, the doors, blasting holes in the walls, letting the air in.

So I lay there, imagining myself violently ventilating my world at least enough to let me go on breathing, and when morning came, I got up and went to work.

It was an impossible situation. Not only were we living way over our means but we had never really resolved the crises of the spring and summer. We simply chose not to talk about them — because if we did talk, we fought.

But even that was something, some kind of contact. When Tinamarie was out with her friends, I didn't have another adult to talk to. For long months Tinamarie was the only grown-up I knew in Austin. I started loitering with Chandler in the nutrition section at the Whole Foods Market on Sixth Street just to pass a few words with other adults; Chandler made friends as easily as his mom did, and I was happy to take the leftovers, or as happy as I could be.

Hope is a necessary quality of the good life. I defy any philosopher to prove otherwise. And hopelessness is an ingredient of most serious depression. In a journal entry from September 26, 2000, I wrote, "I've got to learn to control my feelings more, not to get overwhelmed and become hopeless." It was on my mind a lot, for I had no hope that we could get control of our finances, that we could reverse the ever-widening gulf between us, or that I could ever feel at home in Austin.

Margaret Mohrmann is a fine doctor and a great teacher. I met her at a retreat we spoke at a while back for med school and pre-med students who wanted to learn how to be more humane in their practice. Margaret is an expert on suffering — which is to say she studies it and teaches about it — and her words I took to heart that weekend were about how suffering breaks patterns and shatters wholeness. Tragedy, which is a kind of narrative that leads to despair, results when we can't comprehend how our story fits together anymore, when it seems that the narrative of our lives has shattered into fragments. The intensity of suffering, Margaret said, is directly proportional to our inability to comprehend it.

I thought my life was as shattered into fragments as it could be, that my suffering was as intense as it could possibly get.

Then, just a week after that last journal entry, Tinamarie decided that she'd had enough of me, that she didn't want to be married anymore. She hoped that for the time being I'd be will-ing to stay there in the apartment to be close to Chandler, but she said she couldn't stand the anger and depression that being married to me exposed her to.

Well, she didn't foresee the anger and depression that followed. A few days later, in my journal entry for October 6, just before Chandler's third birthday, I set out to examine some alternatives. I wrote down thirteen possibilities for what I could do to fix this mess.

The first option was "kill myself." Most of the others weren't much cheerier.

The next week, I was headed to Iowa City, Iowa, to be a speaker at a big writing conference. I wept for two hours, all the way up to Waco, where I was flying out. When I got to town, I sat outside my psychiatrist's office until it opened and I could go inside and tell his secretary that I needed to see the doctor that morning, immediately, if possible. She took one look at me and led me back to his office.

After he had me sit down, I told him that if he didn't put me on some kind of medication, I didn't think I would survive the week. He didn't need much convincing. He took one look at me and brought out his prescription pad, where he wrote me a script for sleeping meds and another for the antidepressant Celexa.

I spent most of my time in Iowa City curled up in a fetal ball in my hotel room. I had to go out a few times to give talks, to read from my fiction, to go to dinner — how did I manage those things? — but the rest of the time I just popped pills and hung on. When my literary agent, Jill, called from her tropical vacation to say that she'd just finished reading the manuscript of my novel *Free Bird*, that it was the best book she had read in years, and that she thought we could sell it right away — the sort of news every writer longs to hear, especially one who thinks that being a published novelist could change his life — I told her "thanks," hung up, and curled back into a fetal ball.

On October 14, the wind sent a section of the University of Iowa newspaper flapping across campus and into my hands. It contained comics and the horoscope. Mine, for Scorpio, advised me that if I let go of the ledge I was hanging from, my drop would only be inches instead of into the endless void it seemed like. I actually smiled for a moment. All the same, even in the face of that hopeful prediction, I redoubled my metaphorical grip.

There was one other thing I forgot to mention — I hadn't eaten since Tinamarie told me she was leaving me. That is, I hadn't had any kind of solid food for two weeks. I had lost about twenty pounds off my never-substantial frame. And I don't know how I could have stopped that slide short of extinction except for a tiny miracle that came in the form of Pearson's Drug Store.

In somewhat happier times, the early nineties, when I'd gone up in the summers to study writing at the University of Iowa, I used to go to lunch with my friend Trish at the soda fountain at Pearson's. They made chocolate malts that were among the great delights of the universe. A couple of days into this fetal-curled stay in Iowa City, I recalled those days and decided that even if I was going to waste away and vanish from the planet, maybe it would be okay if I had a Pearson's chocolate malt before I went.

So I trudged up the hill from the campus, weak as the kitten that the other kittens beat up on, made my way into the antiseptic-smelling store, and passed back to the small soda fountain where several people sat around the speckled Formica counter. I ordered a large chocolate malt, thought about it for a moment, and ordered an egg salad sandwich on wheat toast.

With a pickle.

Which was my lunch the next day.

And the next.

If anybody ever tells you not to order that large chocolate malt you've been wanting — let them know that sometimes a chocolate malt can save your life.

That week was probably the darkest time of my life, away from my boys, hurting and alone. But notice how even there in Iowa City, a thousand miles from home, hope came in unexpected ways: in a strange newspaper's prediction that I'd survive; in the memory of friends who loved me; in a chocolate milkshake; and, finally, in the sympathetic ear of a motherly writer who told me I looked like hell and sat on a bench with me one night by the Iowa River while I shed my story, one stranger to another.

They weren't long-term fixes. I was still a long way from finding those. They were more like islands of hope, like the furniture islands that a toddler uses to cruise across the living room, recliner to coffee table to sofa. Without the furniture he'd fall, but with it he can make his wobbly way.

And that, of course, is what I did, and continued to do. The furniture for me was movies, music, my friends, my children, my job, and at last, my church. And as I allowed others to know what was happening with me, I noticed an odd thing: It put me in the strange place of having people come to me with their stories, telling me of their heartbreak and despair.

It seemed to help both of us.

I began to make a point of mentioning in class or in writing projects that I suffered from clinical depression, because as Walker Percy wrote, sometimes just knowing that you aren't suffering alone can be a powerful piece of grace. In his essay "The Man on the Train" (an important source for one of my favorite novels, *The Moviegoer*), Percy imagined two depressed and lonely commuters on a train, one of whom is reading a book about a character who is depressed and lonely:

> The nonreading commuter exists in true alienation, which is unspeakable; the reading commuter rejoices in the speakability of his alienation and in the new triple alliance of himself, the alienated character and the author. His mood is affirmatory and glad: Yes! That is how it is! — which is an aesthetic reversal of alienation.[2]

I knew that experience of "Yes!" which is a rare feeling when you're depressed. It's a feeling of connection when you feel disconnected, a moment of hope that you're not alone. A flash of hope, period.

Anne Lamott wrote that she could believe that something valuable was waiting to be born out of struggle and hardship. "And I especially believe it," she said, "when other people's things are breaking down. When it's my stuff, I believe the direct cause is my bad character."[3]

"Yes!" I said. I'd been in that place of Bad Mind.

When I read a Japanese poem my friend Jane Hirshfield had translated, a poem about night inside a ruined house and the light streaming in through the cracks, I said, "Yes!"

When Bono sang about how "after the Flood, all the colors

came out," it reduced me to tears.

Yes, I thought. Someday maybe it won't be like this. Other people have been where I am. Other people are where I am now.

I am not the lone attraction in this freak show.

So I began offering up my experience to others — as I'm doing now — because sometimes just knowing that you're not suffering alone does make a huge difference. I'm glad I could do that, because in those dark days I didn't have anything much more positive to offer others. But there was something that loomed in front of me, a big piece of furniture, a hope that now seemed like something I wanted to cling to:

God saved me so that I could help other people.

It took me a long time to believe that statement with all its many repercussions and implications, let alone embrace it.

But I don't have to tell you that I believe it now.

solitude

Go, sit in your cell, and your cell will teach you everything.

FATHER MOSES OF SCETE

Way back in the fourth century CE, a group of men and women left cities and towns in the Middle East to withdraw into the deserts and mountain places. Today they're known generically as the Desert Fathers, since most of them were male, and we treat them as saints of the church, which many of them are, actually, although the impulse that drove them out of their culture was a universal one. What they were seeking, Thomas Merton wrote, was salvation, but salvation of a different kind than the world told them it held for them.

The Desert Fathers sought their "true selves," and to find those selves, Merton explained, these men and women "had to reject completely the false, formal self, fabricated under social compulsion. . . . They sought a way to God that was uncharted and freely chosen, not inherited from others who had mapped it out beforehand."[1]

They went to the desert, in other words, for the same sorts of reasons that in 1845 Henry David Thoreau went to spend two years in a tiny cabin he built in the woods outside Concord, Massachusetts: "to live deliberately, to front only the essential facts of life, and see if I could not learn what it had to teach, and not, when I came to die, discover that I had not lived."[2]

In the spring and summer of 2001, I began my own hermitage to take stock, to talk to God, whatever or whoever that might be, and to figure out how to live, because looking back at the first forty years of my life, it was increasingly clear that I hadn't exactly burned up the front nine. The opportunity to retreat came when Tinamarie took Chandler to Thailand, looking for her own set of answers, and my first cell was the tiny one-bedroom place on Woodrow Avenue where I house-sat for Ian, an architect friend of Tinamarie's who was in Spain for a month.

Then for a couple of weeks I moved into a residential hotel in a bad neighborhood in far north Austin, where I lived surrounded by urban poor who couldn't afford to get into an apartment but paid rent for these more expensive rooms because they didn't have the money to put down a deposit. It was an eye-opening look at the cash culture that exists because the poor don't have access to the same sorts of resources middle class families do.

I felt like one of them — and was, in fact, becoming one of them, because even though I earned a good paycheck at Baylor, and *Free Bird* had just sold for a small but welcome advance, I was still paying Jake's child support, and the rest of my money was supporting two households, one on another continent.

In retrospect, it seems more than a little crazy, but that's probably a good description of me in those days. Money was not the only thing about which I was a little deranged.

I was literally living paycheck to paycheck, a PhD with no more money in the bank than the poor families struggling to keep afloat who lived to either side of me, and that was both sobering and scary. I didn't know how they dealt with the pressure. I certainly wasn't dealing with it well.

I cleaned out my bookshelves at my office at Baylor, started selling my books and my movies for five cents on the dollar. When I got caught short of money at the end of the month, I put my electric guitar and amp in the pawn shop, got them out, put them back in again. At last, the clerk at the pawn shop was already filling out the ticket when he saw me come in.

But finally the first check came from my publisher, and when Tinamarie and Chandler came back from Thailand, I got them set up in an apartment, and I found myself a little place a mile or two from downtown Austin in a quiet complex where I was the loudest person.

If you know me, then you know that it was a pretty quiet place.

There was a beautiful big magnolia tree just outside my front door, the floors were Mexican tile, there were built-in bookshelves for my remaining books, and a curtain of green bamboo out my back window magically filtered the sunlight coming through. The place was small — maybe 450 square feet, a third the size of my old house in suburbia, a fifth the size of the house I grew up in. But it was exactly what I needed then.

One's cell should be just big enough to hold you and the few things you cannot do without.

I packed up and moved those things with the help of Raj, who was now my one friend in Austin — a beautiful and funny guy who worked in the nutrition department at Whole Foods

Market. Raj, short for Rajesh, short for Rajeshkumar, had made his own journey, which may have been why he stood by me through so much of mine. He'd been in the ministry as a young man in San Diego, had split up with his wife under heart-wrenching circumstances, and after driving a cab in Santa Barbara and drinking too much to try and forget, he had retreated to Socorro, New Mexico, for six months in 1998 to work in a motel owned by members of his family. It was a painful and powerful time for him. "At night, I would run around in the desert and scream a lot," he told me.

I wasn't a screamer, but I knew that there were things inside me that I needed to get out and that it could only happen for me in my own desert places. At about this time, I remember reading in an apocryphal text, "If you bring forth what is within you, it will save you; if you do not bring forth what is within you, it will destroy you." It's a Zen koan of a saying, and while it touched me, I wasn't sure exactly what it might mean.

What I had inside me was pain and sadness and rage and desperation and a whole lot of negative emotions, and I could see that they would destroy me if I didn't let them out.

But how could they save me?

The thing is, there were other things inside me too, things I wasn't so inclined to credit: love, loyalty, intuition, intelligence, and, surprisingly, increasingly, faith.

Because my retreat was not hermetically sealed, the outside world could still bounce me around pretty good, bruise me like a piece of overripe fruit. Tinamarie and I were still negotiating rough terrain, separated but not yet divorced, and we still broke down into argument far too easily. It was our default setting, and since I was seeing Chandler almost every day, when we handed him off, our flints had plenty of opportunity to strike sparks.

And, on retreat or not, I was still plenty jangled in those first months on my own. When I made a screaming drunken idiot of myself at Tinamarie's birthday party in front of all her cool hippie friends, or when we had a huge fight and she threatened to take Chandler somewhere where he'd never have to listen to me scream at her again, I was right back there in the darkness. On those occasions, I would call my friend Chris, who pastors a church in Houston when he isn't traveling the country, and miraculously — because now I can hardly get through to him to save my life — he always picked up, whatever the hour.

"Hey, buddy," Chris would say. "What's up?"

And I would say something like, "I'm afraid I'm going to do something bad to myself," and he would talk to me calmly and lovingly until I didn't think violence was a possibility anymore.

There's a paradox here, of course, that I recognize. I thought that by pulling myself back from the world, I could save myself. I didn't date, I rarely went out to clubs or movies, I read a lot about religion, I watched DVDs, I practiced my own music, I tried to meditate.

Except, of course, we don't save ourselves. Can't. And, of course, short of living in space or under the ocean, there is no place where we don't have to interact with others.

And except, of course, without Chris and Raj and my friends at Baylor and my boys, I would not have made it through the time in my cell.

This fluid relationship between solitude and society is something I've come to understand about Thoreau over the years as I've thought more about him and his hermitage at Walden Pond. He wasn't setting out on a wilderness adventure; we're not talking about some kind of woolly mountain man here, someone who wanted to be thousands of miles from the nearest city. Thoreau just wanted to get enough distance from the hustle and bustle that he could see things more clearly.

And the Desert Fathers weren't off on their own; they had others of their kind around — the sayings are full of their interactions — and they were close enough to civilization that folks could come and ask them for a blessing or a wise word.

What I came to realize was that *retreat* was more symbol than fact. If I could have pulled back further to a mountain cabin in Wyoming, as I sometimes fantasized, it would not have saved me. In fact, the opposite is probably true.

We are made for each other, you and I. I got things totally wrong when I thought I could fix myself by myself, under my own power and using my own wisdom.

If it had been only up to me, I could have stayed in my apartment, barred the door, and, still, left to my own devices, never gotten it right.

But you know what?

Midway into 2002, after a year or so in my cell, I finally learned what it had to teach me, and it was not about how wise and strong I was going to become.

My whole life I'd sought freedom and control over my own decisions. I thought that I was smart enough, talented enough, determined enough to accomplish whatever I wanted, to make my way in the world wherever my path led.

I thought that if I could spend enough time in my cell contemplating my life, reading theology and history and philosophy, trying to do good, maybe I could figure things out, stand up on my own two feet. In fact, that would be my very strong preference. I didn't need God, or church, or other people to be righteous and whole.

But what my cell and I decided after I'd been thinking that for a year or so was this:

It was the stupidest load of crap the two of us had ever heard.

And so, in the spring semester of 2002, I did a radical, counter-cultural, and counterintuitive thing.

I gave up.

Now this was not a come-to-Jesus moment. Please mark that down. I did not make an altar call and rededicate my life to the Lord, as we said in the Baptist church growing up, or celebrate some sort of ceremony that said I used to be one thing and now I'm another, as we do in the Episcopal church.

What happened was this. One morning, lying in my bed alone, not wanting to get out of it then or ever, I realized that I was finished, done for, like one of those guys in the movies that tells the others, "Go on without me. Save yourselves."

That morning, the covers over my head, I prayed something like this, out loud: "God, I can't make it anymore. I've failed. I don't have the strength. If you want me to live, if you want me to go on, you're going to have to give me the strength. I don't know what that means or what it looks like, but I'm just letting you know: I'm not steering this thing anymore. You've got the wheel. I give up."

When I said those words, I felt an amazing rush of freedom, a strange thing to encounter when you're giving up the rule of your own life and ceding it to someone or something else. But then again it wasn't just any someone or something, any old yoke I was putting on. In the gospel of Matthew, Jesus tells the crowd gathered around him, some of whom must certainly have felt as hopeless as I did, "Come unto me, all ye that labor and are heavy laden, and I will give you rest. Take my yoke upon you, and learn of me; for I am meek and lowly in heart: and ye shall find rest unto your souls. For my yoke is easy, and my burden is light."[3]

It wasn't like Billy Batson saying, "Shazam." No lightning bolt speared out of heaven when I told God I was ready to cede control, and I didn't suddenly become happy, fulfilled, or peaceful, let alone wind up in a costume with a cape.

But I did get out of bed that morning, and the next morning, and the next. And when I got up, I was aware that it was no longer my feet that I was putting weight on, no longer me that held the reins. I told people who wondered how I could keep going with all I was wrestling with, "I just get up in the morning, and I walk on God all day."

It was faith, pure and simple, that I brought forth from within, and as the writer of Thomas suggested, it did save me.

Now, I didn't at first think of myself as a very faith-filled person. The whole time I was walking on God, I still had my doubts, still didn't really expect to survive. But one of the great thinkers in my tradition says to act as if you have faith, and faith will be given to you. And that's what I did — I got up in the morning, and I told people that I was walking on God, and I acted as if I had faith by going on one more day, and I looked up one day, and sure enough, I did.

Of all the things that have happened to me as a result of my depression, all the hardships, all the grace, the most compelling thing I've gained is a living faith in God. Not in the God of my fathers — or of my grandmother, sorry Grandma — but nonetheless, a real, true, living faith that makes me a different person, a hopeful person, that makes me see the world as a different place and makes me want to see that change in others as well.

One of my heroes, the minister and peace activist William Sloane Coffin, has explained faith in this way:

Faith is being grasped by the power of love. Faith is recognizing that what makes God is infinite mercy, not infinite control; not power, but love unending. Faith is recognizing that if at Christmas Jesus became like us, it was so that we might become more like him. . . . Watching Zaccheus climb the tree a crook and come down a saint, watching Paul set out a hatchet man for the Pharisees and return a fool for Christ, we know that our lives too can become channels for divine mercy to flow out to save the lost and the suffering.[4]

Well, amen, as we used to say in the Baptist church — and still say sometimes, at St. James, Austin.

Let it be so.

The cell — or the mountaintop, or Zaccheus the tiny tax-collector's tree, or the dusty track of the Road to Damascus where Paul saw Jesus — these are to be places where we make discoveries about faith, places of transition and transformation. They're not supposed to be places of stagnation, and they're not supposed to be places where we hide in safety from a world that isn't as good as us or sane as us or cool as us or fixed as us.

John Milton — yes, that John Milton, the one you were supposed to read in English lit — wrote contemptuously in his essay opposing censorship, "Areopagitica," about what he called "cloistered virtue"—that is, any attempt by Christians to preserve our sanctity by segregating ourselves or walling ourselves off from the world. As I said, we are made for each other, made to be in community, and if we are going to make a difference in the world, we ultimately have to get up out of our cells and go walking into the world outside, scary as it may be and is.

I still live in the tiniest of apartments now at the Episcopal seminary, and I still have only the barest necessities around—books, of course, and musical instruments, and, okay, far too many DVDs to make Henry David Thoreau comfortable. "Simplicity," he argued in *Walden* and elsewhere, and I have taken his advice, as well as I can, but I do love Hong Kong action movies and "South Park," and if Henry David could watch these things with me, maybe he would forgive.

But as self-contained as it could be, as I could be, I know now that my life is not within these walls. My life is in the seminary, and in my relationship with my sons, in my friendships and my love relationship, in my writing and in my teaching, in my service to the church—now at St. James, the church that saved me, and later, as you read these words, perhaps somewhere else, wherever God and the church have seen fit to put me—and in my service to the world.

I'm still walking on God each and every day, although I'm healthy and sane, and now I recognize my life as a thing of such beauty that I still find myself breaking into smiles at all hours. But now I'm walking further and further into the world.

I don't forget where I've come from. It may be that someday my cell again will have life-changing things to teach me, and it wouldn't surprise me to know that there might again come a season when I'll simply need to sit and listen. In fact, it's good practice in everyday life to take time to sit and listen, to make sure that I'm still headed down the right path, to keep that Internet connection to God blazing fast.

But today and tomorrow, whatever I do and wherever I find myself, I'm trying to be a channel for divine mercy. And because there's not so much need for mercy in here anymore, and lots of need for it out there, off I go.

Don't wait up.

martin

Let us develop a kind of dangerous unselfishness.

DR. MARTIN LUTHER KING JR., "I SEE THE PROMISED LAND"

Last December, December 2004 to be precise, I went to Atlanta for my friend Hunt's ordination ceremony. Went back to Atlanta, I might say, since I lived in Atlanta when I was a small kid, up until midway through first grade, when we moved to Charlotte, North Carolina.

One cold sunny afternoon when we had a little free time, I had Hunt drop me off at the King Center — I wanted to see the burial monument, and the King Center, and Ebenezer Baptist Church, which had been pastored by Dr. King's grandfather and father, and where he himself had served from 1960 to 1968, when he was assassinated. It was while I was talking with Hunt and Roger on the drive over that I realized that I'd actually lived in Atlanta during those last years Dr. King was preaching in that red brick church — those years when he was speaking to the entire world.

The realization that I had been just across town from Dr. King during the climactic years of the civil rights movement was stunning, partly because we then moved from Atlanta to Charlotte, where during my time there, Mecklenburg County, my school district, was embroiled in some of the largest and last court cases over busing and equal opportunities in education.

I had never really thought about why race, prejudice, and tolerance were my hot-button issues, and to be honest, I didn't realize until recently that when I was a small person I was living in mighty times and historic places.

All I knew was that when I was a kid growing up in the South, I didn't like the way most white people treated black people, and that it didn't seem fair. And when we moved back to our ancestral home in Oklahoma, I brought that memory — and that feeling — back with me, and it's stayed with me ever since.

I was watching the first season of "Red vs. Blue" the other night. It's a cartoon series on the Web that dubs in dialogue over scenes from the video game "Halo," and sometimes it's so funny it can make you fall off the couch. In one of the so-called public service announcements on the DVD, a red soldier and a blue soldier were debating the pros and cons of getting a tattoo. The strongest argument against, for me, was this: "Do you remember yourself ten years ago? Do you remember how stupid you were? Is there anything you thought ten years ago that you still think now?"

Okay. I can identify. Certainly there's no piece of body art, nobody's name, I would have wanted inked under my skin ten years ago that I'd still want on my body today. But, as I'm prone to do, I took the question global and had an interesting thought: There was one thing I believed ten years ago that not only hadn't changed, but had gotten stronger, richer, deeper.

Ten years ago, Martin Luther King Jr. was my hero. And

after reading more by him and about him, after teaching his work over and over again at Baylor and in the larger world, after seeing how hard it is to be a Christian and to work for justice, I have to say that I admire him even more.

Thomas Merton has said that the civil rights movement was the highest flowering of Christianity in America, and I think he was right. Not that the temperance movement wasn't a big deal, but still. It gave us Al Capone and bathtub gin; the civil rights movement gave us freedom, or at least a head start toward it. It was the great example of the church at work in the world, and it's an example we have to be constantly reminded of.

Dr. King used to say that if the church didn't involve itself in the day-to-day lives of the suffering, then it would be no better than an irrelevant social club, and frankly, I think some churches today have proven this, have actually pulled back inside their walls with all the other people who know the secret handshake, have settled down to enjoy their own coffee shops and workout clubs and child care, while outside the ark, the world is going under.

Dr. King was far from the first person to argue that the life of the faithful person should be about helping others, of course. He was following the teachings of a group of theologians early in the twentieth century who'd taught that the Social Gospel, as they called it, was the central message of the Christian Testament. And before that, there was, oh, the writer of James in the Christian Testament, who said that faith without works was dead (see James 2:20), and the early Christian church we find described in the Acts of the Apostles, notable for its acts of charity and equity. Then before that, the Hebrew Bible is constantly talking about justice. In fact, the Hebrew word for justice (or righteousness — in the Hebrew Scriptures they're one and the same) is used 157 times in twenty different books of the Hebrew Bible; it's one of the most-used theological words in the Scriptures that Jesus knew and taught from.

And then there was Jesus himself, especially in the gospel of Mark, traveling the countryside healing the sick and feeding the hungry. Let's be clear about this: Jesus didn't heal people because he was on call that weekend. He did it because he grew up in the Jewish tradition of social justice, and because he had come to proclaim the coming of God's kingdom, which for him was symbolized by healing the sick, the blind, and the halt, setting free the insane or the possessed, whatever it was that was going on with those people, from their bondage, and the feeding of the famished. It's what you all should do, Jesus said. And if you do it to any of these people who need help, it's as if you're doing it for me.

So how is it that so many American Christians disagreed with Dr. King when he said we needed to explore both the social and personal levels of sin, when he said that the soul and the body both deserved redemption? How, as King wrote in his "Letter from a Birmingham Jail" could "so many ministers say, 'those are social issues with which the gospel has no real concern,'" how could "so many churches commit themselves to a completely otherworldly religion which made a strange distinction between body and soul, the sacred and the secular"?[1] How could a group of Southern ministers actually have written King the open letter that he responded to in his letter from jail, a letter in which they asked him to stop doing what he was doing?

Why did Dr. King care about those things so much when other American Christians didn't?

The more I read or heard Dr. King's words, the more I learned about Martin the Man and not just Dr. King the Federal Holiday, the more I discovered how the things I most admired about him — his courage, his thirst for justice, his determination — grew directly out of his faith.

And that both puzzled and threatened to inspire me.

During the time I'd left Christianity behind, throughout my twenties and into my thirties, I had no trouble understanding Dr. King if I thought of him as a community organizer or a campaigner for social justice. That made perfect sense to me.

But when I thought of him as Dr. King, the Baptist pastor?

Well, then my head began to hurt.

I didn't want Martin Luther King Jr. to be a Christian.

My problem, really, was this: In the tradition I grew up in, the only social issues ever mentioned from the pulpit were "sin" issues, like horse-racing and liquor by the drink. For us, James' words about faith without works referred to spiritual works like reading the Bible and testifying to the truth and going to church, and not to feeding the hungry.

If Dr. King really was a Christian — and he certainly seemed to think he was — then maybe, just maybe, his was a club I could join. But how to explain the difference between what I saw Christians doing and saying about politics on television and what I saw in Martin? How could two sets of people call themselves Christian when the things they seemed to care about were so different?

Well, the answer, of course, was simple, although I'm not the only one who has wrestled — and wrestles — with the question of Christian identity in America. Journalists and radio interviewers always seem to think that because I'm a devout

Christian I must be a devout conservative evangelical Christian, like that really is the only kind. They're surprised when I tell them that on Saturday nights I like Hong Kong action films and a good margarita, and then on Sunday morning I go to church.

Here's what I tell them, what I learned from Dr. King and people like him: There's more than one way to be a Christian in America.

This shouldn't be a surprise, given the fact that there are like a hundred different Protestant denominations, given the fact that every time you get three Baptists in a room, one of them disagrees with the other two and goes off to start his own church. So here's a simple division: People who are Southern Baptists, Pentecostals, and the other evangelicals that I knew growing up — and they constitute perhaps the largest and most vocal group of Protestant Christians in America — are one kind of Christian. For them, Christianity is primarily about bringing people into joyous new life with God and living that life faithfully until it's time to be lifted into another. Let's call them "salvation" Christians, since salvation is a primary focus for them, and let's be clear that I'm not making a value judgment. Although the churches I grew up in were not right for my faith to grow in, many of the kindest, most wonderful people I know are salvation Christians, including lots of folks in my own family.

Now for Christians like Dr. King, for members of oppressed groups and racial minorities, and for some members of mainline denominations like the United Church of Christ, Presbyterian, and Episcopal Churches, that evangelical impulse might also be present to a greater or lesser extent, but they emphasize justice and how Christ's tradition and his example call for us to be active in addressing the suffering of the world. The Rev. William Sloane

Coffin once preached, "Of course we are to feed the poor, just as did Jesus. In the phrase 'Man does not live by bread alone,' the important word is not 'bread,' but 'alone.' Human rights hardly exhaust the gospel, but they are at the heart of it, not ancillary to it."[2] We might call folks like these "Kingdom" Christians, because they're working to bring the Kingdom of God near.

You can be both kinds of Christian, of course — Brian McLaren and Jim Wallis and other folks I admire tremendously are evangelicals who care about social justice. But they seem to represent a minority, if, I hope, a growing minority, and as I look at the political gamesmanship of the Religious Right, I could almost be back in the pew at the church of my youth.

Dr. King often said that when the final tally was made of the civil rights era, it wasn't the evil deeds of racists and bigots and the Ku Klux Klan that people would lament. In the Birmingham letter, he wrote, "We will have to repent in this generation not merely for the vitriolic words and actions of the bad people, but for the appalling silence of the good people."[3]

I like to think that the white Southern clergymen who wrote the letter that occasioned King's Birmingham response were good men. They thought that Christianity was about saving souls, not about leading marches or making a public spectacle of yourself, and I can believe that they were well meaning, and that they were sincere, because these are my people.

Or rather, they were. I left their camp and wandered in the desert, and then one day I heard a voice calling in the wilderness and I hiked over to check it out.

Which reminds me: When I walked inside the old Ebenezer Baptist Church — for the congregation has moved since Dr. King's day to a beautiful modern church across the street — I could hear Dr. King's voice. In that old red brick building with the narrow windows in the side walls and the baptistery up behind the raised dais where the pulpit and the choir loft are, Martin is still preaching.

Always preaching.

I sat down in a pew and listened to the taped sermon, and as I listened, I imagined him there behind the pulpit, his hand falling to punctuate a point.

And as I looked at that pulpit, I realized that it was tiny. I mean it. Like Munchkin-sized. I walked down to the front of the church, and a closer look confirmed it. I would have towered over that pulpit like Shaq over a tricycle.

Just when I thought nothing else about Dr. King could surprise me, here was this. I would never have chosen him for a game of school-yard basketball.

How did that compact little man change the world? How could someone so small in stature endure all the death threats and physical abuse and thirty trips to jail during his shortened lifespan?

Well, the answer sat me down, right there on the front pew.

Dr. King was indeed a brilliant man with a golden voice and enough courage and charisma to light up a city. But it wasn't the gifts of that short, middle-class black man from Atlanta that lit a moral fire under the segregated South and changed America. It was the faith of the man of God, faith so unshakable that not even death can stop him from preaching.

I have read a lot about Martin Luther King Jr. and I know a little about faith and belief, and I think in some ways he and I were a lot alike. Before either of our transformations, we were people who were seeking good and we were interested in social justice. We studied theology and religion as though we could find our meaning in it, and we believed in God in a stuffy, sort of academic, way. My dear friend Tom Hanks — the one who teaches English at Baylor, not the other one — talked with me some years back about what was for us then a mutual problem. "I'm trying," he said, with the sincerity and intelligence that is that good man's hallmark, "to get more Jesus into my Christianity."

It's hard when you're an intelligent person and your strongest remembrance of Christianity is people who managed to drawl three syllables out of the name "Jesus."

Martin and I believed in God the way you might, say, believe in aluminum. See, there it is, an element on the periodic chart, you can find it in nature, useful in its own way.

But it's one thing to believe in something.

And it's another to have faith in it, to stake your life on it.

In January 1956, Dr. King was in the thick of the Montgomery bus boycott. He had just been jailed for the first time; he had just begun receiving death threats; someone shortly would fire-bomb his house; and he had come to his breaking point. This was not what he had signed on for, what the theological education and the study had prepared him for.

He was ready to give up.

Like I said, I believe in aluminum, that is, that there is such a thing. But when I'm in a plane at 35,000 feet and I look out the window, and what is keeping me there is a wing made of that metal — well then, brother, I have no choice but to have faith.

Martin Luther King Jr. had believed in God his whole life, but had never opened himself to believing in God with his whole heart and soul and strength.

He had never found himself at 35,000 feet before, looking out the window at what might be holding him up.

Late that dark night, as Dr. King submitted himself and confessed his weakness, he received a mystic vision that sustained him through the dangers of all the coming years. As he later told the story about his "kitchen table" conversion, he heard the voice of Jesus say to him: "Martin Luther, stand up for righteousness. Stand up for justice. Stand up for truth. And lo, I will be with you until the end of the world."

Now Dr. King was a supremely rational person. As far as I know, in all the rest of his life, he never had another vision like this. But he never doubted that what he had heard was the voice of Jesus, and that in following those directions, he was doing his work.

I told this story in the first sermon I preached at St. James, shortly after I became an Episcopalian. It was important to me to talk about Dr. King, not just because he's been such a pivotal come-to-Jesus person in my life, but also because he holds a special place in the life of St. James. An icon of Martin hangs on the wall just to the left of the place I like to sit with my friends Liz and Brad and their awfully active toddler, Walker. When I asked Greg about MLK and St. James, he too thought about that icon, which is right over a prayer desk where people can kneel and light a candle in memory or on behalf of someone. Greg said,

For many in our community, these are the eyes they can look into and connect to suffering and sacrifice that is rooted in a faithful joy. MLK represents someone who knew their experience intimately, and for whom they know his. There can be no greater connection. Icons were meant to be windows into the Divine. And this one, for the people here, definitely is.

We celebrate the feast day of Martin Luther King, just as we do the life and work of other saints and apostles of the church. When I say that Martin is a saint, that's not to say he was perfect. First, that's not what "saint" means — in Christian belief, Jesus was the only perfect person, and he had a little more going for him than most of us. No, although Dr. King was admirable, and though he left us a lesson and a life we can emulate, he wasn't perfect.

Some of my students at Baylor are appalled to discover that Martin was unfaithful to his wife. I'm not saying I'm excited about it myself. But if we're all imperfect, then we're all going to fall short somewhere. For me it's just a reminder that Dr. King was human, and remembering that he was as imperfect as I am inspires me to imagine that I too can accomplish the things I'm called to do.

Because, understand, Martin was called to this work. He didn't choose it. He was born into a comfortable middle-class African-American existence, and although he would have been discriminated against his whole life, he could have lived a life of ease, respected by everyone in his community. I think it's important to remember that Dr. King could have lived a safe and satisfied life. In a culture that tells us to get ours where we can and to look out for ourselves first, Martin did not look out for himself.

He didn't seek leadership in the civil rights movement. And when he was elected by his peers to the leadership of the bus boycott in Montgomery, he could have turned it down. From that day on, he lived in daily fear for his life and the lives of his family. His house was bombed, his airline flights had to be specially searched for explosives, and he was threatened in phone calls, letters, and personal encounters.

In one of our less proud national moments, J. Edgar Hoover, director of the FBI, suspected King of being a communist (because why would anybody speak up for the poor unless he was trying to destroy America?) and actually had King put under surveillance, taped, and photographed. On one occasion, Hoover tried to blackmail King: He told Martin that unless he committed suicide, Hoover would send Coretta Scott King audiotape proving his infidelity to her.

But through all that — all the threats to his life, his work, and his reputation — his faith sustained him.

When I left Ebenezer, I walked next door to the pool where Dr. King's tomb is sited, but I didn't really feel his presence there. I'd also been to the Lorraine Motel in Memphis, the place where he was assassinated, and while I found it interesting, it still left me cold.

Then I thought of the words, still echoing back in Ebenezer Baptist Church, still echoing in the world he fought to change.

In the gift shop, I bought a collection of Martin's sermons to give to Hunt as an ordination present. It's in the words where Martin still lives, still moves us, and still inspires us, and I knew Hunt would put those words to good use. He already believes them, and I know that's the hardest part.

Henri Nouwen once wrote, "No minister can save anyone. He can only offer himself as a guide to fearful people."[4]

During his days on earth, that's what Martin was for our nation. But even after he was gone, he was still a guide for me.

And when I teach his work and write about him, it's what I hope he can be for you too: a guide to fearlessly doing what's worth doing in this life.

And a guide to the God who called him in the first place, that very same God who is calling us.

BAPTISM

writing

> Endings are the most important part of stories.
> They grow inevitably from the stories themselves.
> The ending of a story only seems inevitable, though,
> after it's over and you're looking back, as I am now.
>
> DENNIS COVINGTON, *SALVATION ON SAND MOUNTAIN*

I am a Christian writer.

Easy to say now. Once, not so easy.

I used to think you could separate those two things, maybe even should. You know — like "Christian" and "rap." But as you're seeing, this book is a record of things I was ultimately mistaken about.

I am a Christian writer.

Slowly, reluctantly, I came to both acknowledge and announce this truth, but it has been a long and not always pleasant journey, and I remain a little leery of the label, for truly I mean something a little different by "Christian" than, say, Pat Robertson does when he says it. And yet, as Walker Percy noted some years ago in an essay he called "How to Be an American Novelist Despite Being Southern and Catholic," I too must ruefully accept that I may have more in common with a Robertson or Jerry Falwell than with, say, a Donald Trump or Larry Flynt, and if I have to be identified with one culture or the other, I may have no real choice in the matter.

Let me establish at the outset that I don't resist the label of Christian writer because I feel threatened in terms of my career or the acceptance of the reading public, for certainly that would be a reason, at least. But it's not a reason: More than any time in my life, there is a spiritual hunger everywhere I look, a hunger for connection, for some sort of ultimate meaning. Finally our society seems to have grasped what Dr. King often said in sermons forty years ago: "The great problem facing modern man is that the means by which we live have outdistanced the spiritual ends for which we live."

Now we seem to have at least nominally accepted the truth of this pronouncement, and the results actually border on the bizarre. We live in a culture in which the figure of the Dalai Lama is perhaps more immediately recognizable than that of his disciple Richard Gere, in which books about the life of the spirit and the coming apocalypse clamber over each other to ascend the best-seller lists. At a time when religious writing is one of the few growth areas in the book industry, embracing my religion could actually be a good career move.

Fear of failure is not why it took me so long to overcome my reluctance to accept the mantle of Christian writer.

Partly I suppose I was responding to the stereotype that most people summon up at the words "Christian writing," because I have always been, frankly, an artistic chauvinist. Christian writing for the most part is still, with some notable exceptions, acknowledged by editors, readers, and critics to be an artistic ghetto, and I do not care to be forced inside its walls. Thomas Keneally wrote in *Schindler's List*, "It is a risky enterprise to have to write of virtue," and Christian writers prove the truth of this maxim daily.

Certainly there are twentieth-century writers who professed Christianity and produced great works of fiction. I have long admired the holy Catholic trinity of Graham Greene, Flannery O'Connor, and Walker Percy, and gradually began to see that even for a low-churcher, as I was raised, there were fine literary models like Bret Lott, Lee Smith, and Dennis and Vicki Covington.

Although this is more difficult to admit, I had trouble thinking of myself as a Christian writer because most of my life I have not thought of myself as a particularly good Christian, or even much of a Christian at all. I suppose that during much of my twenties and thirties I would have called myself a "cultural Christian" like some nonreligious Jews think of themselves as culturally Jewish — it brings to mind Anne Lamott quoting a comedy routine by Jonathan Miller: "I'm not a Jew. I'm Jew-ish."[1] Well, I was Christian-ish, and struggling with my upbringing in a church that still convinced me sometimes in visceral ways beyond conscious thought that I could never measure up to the demands of an angry God. For let's face it, at least in the eyes of the world, I'm something of a mess: However much you might admire my teaching and my writing, I have a solid record of failure in relationships and in commerce. I want to do better; I have been called, I know, to better things, but who am I, those old voices say, to claim to be a worthy spokesperson for the words God gives me?

That's the world talking, I know, and my old self. In God's eyes, I'm as special as they come. But I haven't always seen that.

I have been a writer since I was about four years old. When I was younger, I tended to write about clowns and firemen, but if you look at the literary productions of my adult life, you'll find an awful lot of stories about broken people — mostly men, but some women, some children — who are hoping that someday something will change for them, that things will get better. Over the course of about forty short stories and some bad novels that didn't quite pan out, I found myself playing with the same kinds of characters and themes, over and over, as though something were broken in me as well, which of course it was.

I liked the stories I was writing, and they were good stories — people kept publishing them, anyway — but if I hadn't discovered the fiction of Richard Ford and Walker Percy in my late twenties, I think I might have decided that I was writing about people that nobody else could identify with, which struck me as strange, since I knew that the people I wrote about existed.

I knew it because they were people exactly like me, lost and looking for home, like E.T., and about as useful on this planet as E.T., when it came right down to it.

So I reconciled myself to being a niche writer — a writer who wrote well about a certain kind of person, let's say. But the thing is, sometimes I would hear from people who had read my stories in the small magazines and journals where they appeared, and they were writing to thank me. They'd tell me that my story had touched them, because they'd seen their own lives in those pages.

And sometimes, which would freak me out more than anything else, they would tell me that the stories had given them hope or had helped them turn a corner.

How could this be? I asked myself. I didn't have much hope myself in those days. How did it get into the stories? But these stories about broken people were not static; sometimes the broken people didn't stay broken. Sometimes there was a spark of something divine that gave them another chance, even when they didn't deserve it.

I was raised in the church, and I've got the King James Version of the Bible in my blood. I thought I would know if what I was writing was Christian. In those stories, I wasn't talking about God, exactly.

And yet, despite all this, as I looked at my own stories, I began to see that they were deeply religious (if down deep at the core instead of peanut butter spread across the surface). There's a name for the idea of "something moving in the universe that gave them another chance, even when they didn't deserve it," for example. In Christian parlance, we call it "grace," and what we mean by it is the gift of undeserved and unmerited love by and connection to God.

In one of my stories, a son forgives his abusive father while sitting at his father's deathbed by remembering how his father taught him to play baseball when he was a kid. In another, the nagging love of a friend for a suicidal ex-con refuses to let him do away with himself. In another, a girl in a small-town church discovers that people and institutions can fail you, but that God is bigger than the ways we fail one another.

Grace, forgiveness, connection, faith, and hope were inside every one of these stories I was writing while I was running from God, and only the fact that I was the author of them all kept me from making the obvious connection. I was a writer trying to tell a beautiful story about a character in crisis, but if I'd been reading them from the outside, those theological themes would have been the first things I would have noticed, as they were when I first began reading the beautiful and powerful stories of Andre Dubus, the late great Catholic short-story writer.

Since I started publishing novels in 2002, it's been a lot more obvious, and I've been a little less reticent about admitting it. My first novel, *Free Bird,* is simultaneously a comic road novel and a spiritual quest filled with sacraments; its climax is a confession, an actual I-have-sinned confession to a Catholic priest, for crying out loud. My second novel, *Cycling,* is about a search for grace in a broken world. The main character is as screwed up as I used to be, and yet, at the end of the book, he actually uses that word "grace." And the novel I finished most recently, *Sanctuary,* which may be in print as you read this, is the story of a lapsed Catholic, a doctor whose desire to heal and be healed encompasses both the physical and the spiritual.

Okay, you got me.

I admit it.

I am a Christian writer.

Back around the time Chandler was born, it had finally become clear to me. As I looked over my body of work, not counting the stuff about clowns and firemen, I discovered over and over in my stories the great Christian themes of suffering, forgiveness, grace, and redemption. My characters were scarred and sometimes broken by life, but somewhere in each story I realized that I presented them with the possibility for reconciliation and redemption. And so despite the fact that many of the people I wrote about would not even be welcome inside a Christian bookstore as paying customers, I began to suspect the truth.

My teacher Robert Olen Butler, a Pulitzer Prize-winning author of short stories and himself some sort of a Catholic, likes to tell writers, "If you're going to be a God, be a merciful God." What I believe he means by that is this: As a benevolent author, it is my responsibility to extend the same grace to my characters that I believe has been extended to me. That is to say, in every story a writer should present the possibility for redemption, even if it is ultimately and tragically rejected by the main character. And so I have; and so I will. All of this has made me recognize my writing — if not always myself as the author of it — as deeply Christian.

In 1998, I got a better understanding of that relationship between belief and art. It was in the fall of that year that I first talked with Andre Dubus. At the time, he and I shared the same agent, and, I came to see, much more besides. I had long admired him as a short-story writer of incredible literary talents, a creative artist who shaped the world through words; I had recently come to admire him as a man of faith. But as we talked more and I got to know him better, I comprehended an even more important correspondence between us. Not only did we have in common faith and artistry but Andre had also made more than his share of personal mistakes, was possessed in fact of a personal life just as disastrously messy as my own — kids and ex-wives and he was working out of a wheelchair; I at least could try to flee on two feet. And yet this same imperfect, deeply scarred human being also brought me stories of transcendent beauty and deep faith. It was a puzzle, if one that he himself resolved.

On the day before he died, Andre said to me, matter-of-factly, as though he were not about to change my life, "I never know the answer to the question about Catholicism and my writing. I've been a Catholic all my life. That's just the way I see the world. We all share in the universals, but my worldview is shaped by my being a Catholic, just like yours is shaped by being a Baptist," which is what I sort of was in those days.

No one had ever put it to me in that way before, although it made perfect sense. There was, in fact, no denying that, for good and ill, he was right. It was a vision of truth.

You write what you write because of who you are.

And is who you are demonstrated by what you write?

Well, duh.

And so I caved in, not precisely like Paul on the road to Damascus, perhaps, although it was with the huge realization that maybe I wasn't just Christian-ish, for I am willing now to proclaim that yes, I am both a believing Christian and a literary writer, that the two identities are in fact one, that I embrace this union of sometime opposites as necessary to the vocation God has given me.

I am willing now to proclaim that I am on a quest for grace in this world, and that grace manifests itself for me in many ways. I find it in the laughter of my sons, in the diamond-dusting of sunshine glinting across a mountain lake, in the stories and words of writers I admire, and my hope is to reflect some of that grace through my own stories.

Perhaps those stories will never convert sinners to belief in Jesus Christ as their personal Lord and Savior, because you know what? They're not written to do that. But if I can create worlds that mirror God's redemption, forgiveness, and love, if I show people the hope there can be in a broken world, I think I am doing the job I am called to do.

Now that I am a seriously religious person, I find that I have to watch out, in fact, that I don't accidentally preach when what I'm supposed to be doing is telling a story. There is a time and place to preach, but generally it's not while you're writing a scene for a novel or short story or film or stage play. When you believe something strongly, whether it's in free trade or home brewing or God Almighty, the temptation is always to try to say too much, to convince readers by arguing with them directly, by trying to draw them into a confidence like a drunk trying to drag a pretty girl onto his lap. It's fair to say that usually if you haven't created a relationship with your reader yet, you're just going to get slapped in the face and left alone.

My students, God bless them, sometimes think that preaching is the whole point — that writing fiction is about converting the world (or that small subset of it reading their words) to their point of view, or about demonstrating their hard-earned wisdom to a crowd (or that small subset of a crowd) of seekers clustered at their feet. And it most assuredly is not. No one's going to listen to the sermon if you haven't told an interesting story.

Some of my literary heroes thought at length about the relationship between art and faith, so we enter an ongoing conversation. Novelist and historian Shelby Foote, for example, had a long-standing literary argument with his dear friend Walker Percy about writing fiction that had elements of faith in it: "Didacticism is death to the creative urge," he wrote Percy in 1951. "A story had better be told for its own sake."[2]

Thomas Merton would have agreed that the art came first. "A Catholic poet," he wrote, "should be an apostle by being first of all a poet, not try to be a poet by being first of all an apostle. For if he presents himself to people as a poet, he is going to be judged as a poet and if he is not a good one his apostolate will be ridiculed."[3]

Foote and Merton were both right; art typically succeeds or fails on its own merits. When my creative writing students tell me their ideas for a story, the best stories invariably follow when they describe an interesting situation or character, the worst when they tell me they want to write a story about an issue or an idea, want to convert the reader to a particular point of view.

Foote, in his thirty-year epistolary dustup with Percy over how and why to write, made his point well, yet he never seems to have completely understood what Percy was saying in return, and ultimately, demonstrating in novels like *The Moviegoer, Love in the Ruins,* and *The Thanatos Syndrome*: that you could write a good novel using dramatic situations and employing interesting characters and still have it *say* something, have it call the world to account. Percy actually agreed with Shelby Foote that it was more important to write well than to preach. Still, he wrote, "I do not conceive it my vocation to preach the Christian faith in a novel, but as it happens, my world view is informed by a certain belief about man's nature and destiny which cannot fail to be central to any novel I write."[4]

There it is again: worldview. We all write from our world-views. Stephen King was shaped by some long-ago events to write scenes and stories that explore the dark side of existence, Barbara Kingsolver to dissect the structures of power that underlie our lives.

Who I am and what I've seen and what I believe has shaped what I write, too; there's no denying that. Because it's one of the things that I find most compelling in life, I write about relationships — between family members, between those who are or who used to be in romantic relationship, between humans and the divine. Because the past has pursued me my whole life — and, of course, because I grew up in the South — I write about characters who grapple with their pasts, with family, with traumatic events, with bad decisions. Because I've wrestled with depression and despair for much of my life, I tend to write about people who have been broken by their relationships and by their past. And because I'm a person of faith and because I want to be a merciful God, the characters in my stories may be broken, but there's also hope for them, the kind of hope I was writing about long before I knew I might find it for myself.

My friend Rodger Kamenetz says that the function of the writer today is to redeem our most important words for a broken world. A writer might have to write an entire poem — an entire novel — to recreate the meaning of "love," or "forgiveness," or "grace" for a reader. But if it is well done, the word will shine through in all its glory, reclaimed from centuries of lazy or malicious misuse.

Both Merton and Percy wrote of the difficulty of finding language when so many of the words that matter have been reduced to meaninglessness: Love. Courage. Heroism.

Merton argued that "the more earnestly we hope to tell the truth, the more secretly we are convinced that we will only add another lie to all the others told by our contemporaries. We doubt our words because we doubt ourselves — and woe to us if we do not doubt our words and ourselves!"[5] Yet, despite the doubt, despair, and difficulty, that is what the writer is called to do, today more than ever, especially if he is going to call the stories he writes "Christian."

When I wrote my novel *Free Bird*, I didn't set out to do any more than tell a gripping story about Clay Forester driving across the country to attend his father's funeral in Santa Fe. But

Free Bird illustrates the concepts of faith or hope or forgiveness far better than any dictionary definition could. When Clay decides to get busy living instead of busy dying, as Stephen King describes it in *The Shawshank Redemption*, it's exactly what Rodger Kamenetz was talking about — the story has redeemed a part of our language that had lost its immediacy, its power to make us feel and help us understand.

Or so, at least, people tell me, and that is my fervent hope. That's why it's almost impossible to say what a novel is about — as Bob Butler says, a novel is about the experience of reading it, about, when you get to the end, how you feel, what you've learned, how you've changed in response to the ride you've taken.

That's why I think story is such an important part of communicating ultimate meaning, and why I fight against bad storytelling: God is in the details, not in the bald argumentation. Jesus told good stories, and the only reason he ever explained them was because his disciples were numbskulls.

There is much more to say but we can put down roots here. Robert Frost used to say of writing that it reminded him that there is always something worth the doing, that to write well is to make a momentary stay against confusion.

When you read my stories, fiction or nonfiction, I hope you'll find a beautiful story, well told, with characters you can identify with. I also hope you'll find some grace, take away some meaning from what you read, and maybe even feel that you've been drawn closer to God in some way.

If you do, even if only in a small way, then I've done my job. All of it.

Because, you see, I am a Christian writer.

in the valley

Out of the depths, oh LORD, I call to you.

PSALM 130

The first time I went to the Trampas Valley in the Sangre de Cristo mountains was in the summer of 1999. Some friends had let us use their time-share in Santa Fe for a week, and it was a generous and sweet-spirited gesture on their part, although the trip was a hard and often painful one, a preview of how my family and I would spend the next full summer in Santa Fe in ways both positive and negative.

Chandler was never a traveling baby. This is a bitter irony, considering in years since he's traveled happily all over the country — and the world. But for his first few years of life, he fought the child seat — what we called the Buddy Seat — for dear life, back arched, grabbing for release, and screaming bloody murder to get out once we got him strapped in.

Although I knew rationally that he wasn't in pain or suffering more than containment, his screams were elemental. I still can't listen to children screaming, whatever the reason.

Those screams could tear the protective covering off your

heart and your soul, and if you had to listen to them for hours on end, as we had to do to go anywhere outside Waco — which is to say, anywhere worth going — they tore the protective covering off your sanity as well.

In fact, one time coming back from Dallas in rush-hour traffic, with an hour of Chandler screaming behind us and at least two more hours in front of us, Tinamarie and I both lost it. Because we couldn't scream back at him, we screamed at each other, and things went from there. Before I knew it, we were hurling elemental obscenities at each other like people about to cut each other up with razors, and her invectiveness added on to what Chandler was doing pushed me over the edge.

I can see now how people just like you or me do horrible things and then, to try to explain why, say things like "I snapped."

Because that's what happened to me.

I snapped.

In the midst of this surging rush-hour exodus, I somehow yanked the car across three lanes of traffic, over the median separating the access road from I-35, across the access road, over the curb, and into the middle of a vacant lot, Tinamarie and me and Chandler all screaming at the top of our lungs, if for very different reasons.

We stopped dead in the middle of this vacant lot, dust boiling up from underneath our wheels, and I threw the door open with some vague intention of walking out of this life and into another one — or, at least, of walking straight ahead and never looking back.

But I got about 150 feet away, and I could feel the eyes on me, and, being 100 miles from home and all, I began to feel faintly ridiculous about my resolve to walk to Waco or wherever it was I was planning to end up.

But that's the kind of screaming I'm talking about, the kind that could make you that kind of crazy, and it's the kind we had for hours on end as we drove out of Waco in the middle of the night, hoping Chandler would be asleep — he wasn't — or would soon fall asleep — he didn't.

It was no wonder that when we got to Santa Fe the next day I had a horrifying case of either poison ivy or some kind of dermatitis — hysterical eczema, you might call it — all over my body. I tend to break out when I'm pushed over the edge, exhausted beyond belief, and during my depressed years, especially after Chandler came, my arms, legs, or torso were often covered with itchy, painful rashes, which didn't do much to encourage a sunny disposition.

I don't remember much about our week in Santa Fe, although I know Tinamarie has pictures somewhere, which indicates that we did things. I remember mostly the nights when I lay awake, my rash keeping me from sleeping, and my unfocused but very potent anger.

My life was hard enough. I couldn't sleep under the best circumstances. My friends had made a substantial sacrifice so that we could have some fun.

And if anybody was having fun, it wasn't me.

We had agreed, though, that I could take the car off one day all by myself and head for the high mountains. After reading some things, I had chosen to do the Trampas River hike because it was high — the trail began at 9,000 feet and ended at a set of mountain lakes at 11,500 — and long — the round trip was around twelve miles, a very strenuous one-day trek. Over the years I've met many people doing it as an overnighter as I'm coming back down the same day I went up.

I also chose the hike because my guide book said that the trail was one of the best designed and maintained in New Mexico.

So: high, hard, but possible.

At that point, I thought it would be nice to wrestle with a challenge that was only extremely challenging.

On my free day, I took the old road that runs from Santa Fe to Taos. On the way, I passed through Truchas, where Robert Redford filmed *The Milagro Beanfield Wars*, through the tiny village of Trampas with its beautiful little church, and then drove the long forest road just north of the village, through dry cedar forests and up into cool aspen stands with the white-rippled Trampas River always on my right, either visible, or, at times, far below me, so far in fact that it was better if I didn't look over that way. Eight miles or so I went, past tiny houses and graveyards and churches, climbing higher and higher, leaving the world of man behind.

It came as no real surprise, though, that as I got out of the car and I followed the trail into the Pecos Wilderness, some things had changed since the last time the guidebook writer had passed through. Early on, before I could even get into a good rhythm, I had to climb over a huge spruce fallen across the trail, then another, then a third.

It was not such easy going after all.

Beauty was bountiful, the river was burbling in the voice of God as it fell down the mountainside, but I found myself huffing over or around individual fallen trees, then stands of trees, and finally acres of blowdown.

Sometime the winter before, something big had moved across these mountainsides and knocked down forests, literal forests, splayed and strewn them like a kid emptying out a box of toothpicks, and now, if I was going to go on, I was going to have to somehow get across them.

So I did. At one point, an entire mountainside of spruce trees had been knocked down, the trail was completely gone, and I simply clambered across acre after acre of shattered trees. My heart was pounding in my chest—just walking becomes a challenge at 10,000 feet—and I could feel the weight of my pack unbalancing me every time I jumped from trunk to trunk. One misstep, one slip, and I could wind up with a broken ankle or worse. I wiped my face, tried to catch my breath, and kept jumping, swaying, getting my balance.

It was hard going. I thought over and over, "I should go back."

And then, in the upper reaches of the trail, as I moved from the Canadian Life Zone to the Hudsonian Zone, the vegetation changed from giant spruce to hardy bristlecone pines and subalpine firs, the trail reappeared from under fallen giants, and then at last a vista of sparkling blue opened up in front of me, one of the Trampas Lakes.

Ringed by high ridges about five hundred feet higher than the lakes, bordered by tenacious tundra plant life, the Trampas Lakes may have been hard to reach, but I knew immediately I'd found one of the sacred places of the world. I made my way to the far end of the farther lake, took a seat on a boulder, listened to the water lapping against it, closed my eyes.

In some way I couldn't explain, I was happy.

I felt healed. In fact when I came back to the condo in Santa

Fe that evening, Tinamarie looked at me, made an odd face, and said, "Did you know your poison ivy is gone?"

It felt like I had come home.

Even in all the years that I couldn't say the word God, I believed there was a God, and that the best place for me to find him was outdoors. I'd been drawn to the outdoors my whole life. I loved to work outside with Grandpa Chuck, to go fishing with my Grandpa Orval, to go on long bike rides alone. When I was a kid, we visited the Smoky Mountains in the summers to escape the heat of the Carolina plains, although it's hard to know if God is trying to speak to you when your brother Jeff is throwing up all over you and your souvenir tomahawk in the back of the station wagon.

It was in the early 1990s, after I had moved to Waco to teach at Baylor, and long before I was hatching plans to off myself in responsible ways, that I began escaping several times a year to the mountains. When I first started, it was the Sacramento Mountains in southeastern New Mexico, near Cloudcroft or Ruidoso, the closest alpine terrain to central Texas. Later, as I saw — felt — how important the mountains were to my health and well-being, I traveled to others — the Sangre de Cristos in northern New Mexico, the Colorado Rockies, the Wind River Range and Tetons in Wyoming, the Cascades in Oregon, and back to the Smoky Mountains, this time without my brother.

Mostly I went by myself, put up a tent, hiked, read, journaled, climbed ridges to see what was beyond, waded in chilly streams or took dips in mountain lakes. Sometimes, I went entire days without saying a word or without hearing one spoken by another human being.

I felt then that what I was doing was keeping myself sane.

I know now that I was keeping myself alive.

In the mountains, in the trees, in the burbling water, I felt a presence, a Presence. I saw a greater good, was surrounded by a beauty that could keep my inmost ugliness at bay.

I knew, even when I couldn't say it, that God was there, and that God was speaking to me, and that I needed to listen.

One of the first things I learned about being Episcopalian was why I found God in nature, in the works of human beings, and in other places besides the Bible. I had grown up in a Christian theology that sees the world as a fallen place, full of evil, and given over to Satan. If you see the world in this way, then you imagine its brokenness has a cosmic dimension: The sinful world is such a mess because that's all it could be.

Episcopalians believe in sin — although not, I confess, all the sins I believed in as a young Southern Baptist — but we don't believe it's the world that's sinful. We believe the world is good, because God created it. All of it.

Sin comes into the world because we rebel against God, against God's purposes for us, and we don't do it just because we were born or because the devil holds our mortgage. We sin because it's our nature to be proud and selfish, to want things for ourselves. But it's not the fault of the world. The great Celtic theologian Pelagius went around the block with St. Augustine on the concept of original sin, and I still find his argument moving and compelling, even though, by most reckonings, he lost the argument: "Deeper than any wrong in us is the light of God, the light that no darkness has been able to overcome."[1]

The Anglican tradition has roots in both the Roman tradition — the tradition of Catholic church history and theology — and in the Celtic tradition. It's the latter tradition that gives us the teaching of the innate goodness of Creation and our ability to connect with God through it. The priest and poet Gerard Manley Hopkins wrote, "The world is charged with the grandeur of God," and that's how both the old Celtic way and the modern Anglican way would have us believe. It's a way of looking at the world that lets me know that the tingle I'm feeling when I listen to Radiohead or Coldplay or Bruce Springsteen is something sacred, that a great work of art can reveal God, perhaps in ways I never imagined before. Incarnational theology tells me that when I see created beauty like mountains, rivers, or a circling eagle riding thermals in an upward spiral, it can and should draw me closer to God. As Urban Holmes says, "To know creation is to know God for those who can look beyond the landscape to the inner reality."[2]

It's not pantheism that we're talking about here — the idea that God *is* everything — but it is a theology of incarnation — that God created everything and is *in* everything, if only we have eyes to see. In 2002, on a book tour that took Chandler and me from New Mexico to North Carolina — the reverse of the journey along I-40 the hero makes in my novel *Free Bird* — Chandler, back in his Buddy Seat, where he sat drumming along with the Beatles, suddenly and out of nowhere said, "Jesus is here in the car. He's in my drumstick. He's in my Buddy Seat. He's everywhere. He's God."

"Uh-huh," I said. I looked back to make sure he wasn't levitating.

He wasn't. That didn't happen until we reached the mountains.

Every religious tradition I know of believes that there are holy places — "thin places," as the Celts had it — where God and world are only just separate. Over thousands of years, people have made pilgrimages to those places — to Mecca and Jerusalem, to shrines and rivers, to any place where they felt the touch of the divine — and although I didn't know it, I was making a pilgrimage too, each time I traveled into the high places.

My most favored — if not, perhaps, my most favorite — of all these beautiful places is the Trampas River, where I've come back year after year, in times of darkness and in times of light. I've come by myself, with family, at times when I was the only person at the trailhead, and when I shared it with many others. I've hiked in rain and in hail and in dry heat where dust coated me inside and out, when there was snow in the high passes and when a dozen kinds of wildflowers were in rainbow bloom. I've climbed straight up the mountains to walk the high ridges with curious mountain goats.

For too long a time, the Trampas River was one of the few places I knew I could reliably touch God — or that God could touch me.

And so I came back, even in the darkest of dark times, in the same way that a penitent comes to a holy place, because I wanted one thing above all.

I wanted to be healed.

By the summer of 2001, I had suffered and made others suffer. I had lost my family, most of my money, and come close on several occasions to losing my life. And although I was now living alone in my own small apartment, I still felt that my life was totally out of my control.

That June I went to the mountains and pitched my tent at the Trampas River trailhead for a couple days of hiking and reading and thinking.

It was one of those hard times when you can see that things might improve — and yet they haven't. In some ways, it was harder than abject hopelessness, because I could see a sliver of hope that hadn't been there before — and yet that sliver was all I could see, not the whole glowing full moon, and I was starting to lose my patience.

It was like getting a rejection letter that praised your work and said that they had almost accepted it, that they had agonized over the decision, that next time things might be very different.

Except, if you're getting a rejection notice, no matter how hopeful it reads, bottom line: It's still a rejection notice.

This is from my journal for June 25, 2001, my first day on the trail:

It's about 10:30 in the morning. I am hiking at around 9,000 feet above sea level in the Sangre de Cristo mountains, and the song I can't get out of my head is the old Bo Diddley song, "Who Do You Love?"

I think, actually, it's the George Thorogood version, but all the same, one might rightfully ask, "Wha huh?"

I should be lost in the birdcalls, in the lush wet greenery under my feet and all around, in the hot sun beating on my head and face, in the exertion of climbing this ladder to the sky. But then, this is my problem, has always been my problem: My brain has no effective Off switch. It runs its own programming, whether I'm supposed to be focusing my thoughts in prayer, submerging them in meditation, or extinguishing them in sleep.

This is why I have come to the mountains, again, as always, looking for peace. For quiet.

But more, this time, I've come looking for a miracle, because I have come to believe that my life depends on it.

My head is full of words, and I don't know where they all come from:

Be still and know that I am God.

You have to lose yourself to find yourself.

Who do you love?

I thought that if I lost myself I would find myself. And I have lost myself, but I haven't found anything yet. I've just gone on to begin losing everything else.

Although it was broad daylight when I put those words on paper, this is clearly the record of another dark night of the soul.

How long, I wondered, would I have to try to do better, to try to believe, and not have something change?

I probably wrote this journal entry at around 10,000 feet, about a mile and a half into the hike. That's the point by which I'm usually gasping for my second wind and looking for a good place to sit and look for it. Even that early in the hike, I can feel the sweat beading on my face and forehead, and my backpack has started to weigh 150 pounds. The best place to sit down is on a large granite rock near the bottom of a hillside covered by an avalanche slide. Usually I stop there, get a drink, change out of the long-sleeve shirt I put on back in the tent when I was freezing. Sometimes I plant a beer or Diet Coke in the frigid river for the afternoon return. And sometimes, when I've got something on my mind, I take out my journal and write.

I didn't walk or write my way into any solutions that day,

although it was a beautiful hike. I came home that evening, tired and hungry, turned in early, slept hard in the chilly night.

I didn't hike the next day. Instead, I spent the whole day trying to dam the frigid and fast-flowing Trampas River, one river-smoothed rock at a time. I had camped right at a bend of the river, and in front of my tent the river swirled off the bank, then in a slow clockwise circle before heading down the mountain.

I'm not sure exactly what compelled me to put on my Tevas and sink my feet into the numbingly cold water — or to continue to stand and move and stack rocks in that chilling river hour after hour, until the numbness had turned to painful needles in my feet and hands — but that's exactly what I did.

Maybe it was just that what I was doing was tangible effort with a tangible product. For all the frantic dogpaddling I'd done in the river of my life over the last year, I couldn't see that I'd gained any ground — if anything, I'd drifted on around the bend from where I thought I'd camped.

But as the sun rose high and shone straight down on my little corner of the Trampas, I toted big rocks and small stones, heaped them in a straight line, added course on course. The water pressure grew more powerful in the confined channel left for the river to flow unimpeded so I had to struggle to stay afoot as I walked back and forth. Gradually, I could see that I had raised the level of the river behind my dam, created a sort of wading pool in the slow clockwise swirl in front of my tent.

I wanted more — I stacked heavy stones, tried to stop the flow of the river, got knocked off my feet, and felt my whole body go numb as I splashed down.

It couldn't be done. I knew that on a rational level. There was too much water, and, like the grace of God, it never stopped coming, and try as I might through my own efforts to push or pull or restrain it, it was going to batter its way through eventually.

And so it did. It knocked down my top layer of stones as I watched, and when I awoke in the morning, I found a huge breach in the dam where the river had found its course again and pushed my feeble objections out of the way.

The New Mexico mountains are not the highest, or the wettest, or the greenest I've visited in the last ten years. But what I've always loved about them is the incredible contrast to the arid sand-swept plains below. Within the space of just a few miles, you rise from the Sonoran Desert Zone to green, to trees, to water in abundance.

In the New Mexico desert, you can see signs of water — in my travels through the state, I often cross dry creek beds spread out across a dry valley floor or see colorful sandstone formations shaped by wind and rain or see arroyos eroded from the sandstone by some powerful flow — but rarely the water itself.

But that doesn't mean that it isn't there. And in fact, if you just turn your head in another direction, relocate your body a few miles, you'll find it everywhere, so plentiful and so powerful that it can move you.

I went to bed that second night on the Trampas tired and cold and happy as the river sang and burbled just outside my tent.

I had never expected to defeat the river or to turn it to my own purposes anymore than I think Jacob thought he could drop that angel two falls out of three.

I just wanted to touch it — and for it to touch me.

And it did, enough, at least, to last me awhile when I came back down to that desert land, where I could only remember the presence of water by its absence, could only remember the joy of it sweeping me off my feet and singing to me in my sleep.

simplicity

*If we are fools enough to remain at the mercy of
the people who want to sell us happiness, it will be
impossible for us ever to be content with anything.
How would they profit if we became content?*

THOMAS MERTON, *CONJECTURES OF A GUILTY BYSTANDER*

L et's imagine that a herd of hungry elephants thunders into
a poor farming village in Africa. They march through the
compound, ravaging the crops, stuffing themselves with the
very stuff the farmers need to live. And when they are done,
they tromp away to their next meal, leaving the tiny ruined
humans to try to survive as best they can.

Oh well, we might say. Sad story. But they are elephants,
after all. Of course they're hungry — they're enormous. They're
at the top of the food chain. They have to eat more than their
share.

But do they? Is it good for anyone — elephants included — to
be this hungry?

A few years ago, I was helping Chris with a book he wrote
on the Enron debacle, *The Tao of Enron*. Since Chris knows a lot

of people in Houston and is a pretty well-known pastor, he had even managed to get an interview with Enron CEO Ken Lay himself, and as Chris reports it, they had a good conversation about a lot of different things.

But shortly before it was time to send the book off to the publisher, Ken Lay withdrew his permission to run the interview.

"Why?" I asked Chris.

"I don't know, Bro," he said, "but I think he was upset about the chapter on simplicity."

"So," I said, trying to get my mind around this, "he didn't mind the chapters where we implied that he was a bad Christian and a crook and a cheat, but the chapter about how people should get by with less set him off?"

"I guess so," Chris said.

We had written a long chapter suggesting that what had happened with Enron demonstrated how America's interest in acquisition had gotten out of hand and was certainly unChristian, and for someone who owned a bunch of houses and a whole lot of stuff, maybe it was too much. I don't know — he and I didn't talk about it. In any case, it didn't run, and Chris's book was fine without it, and I just packed it away as further evidence that we Americans have gone terribly wrong in our love of things over people.

Because we have.

Let's start with some uncomfortable truths: America represents just 5 percent of the world's population. That is, only one out of every twenty people on earth is an American. Oh, but we are a hungry little person. We consume one-fourth of the world's resources. We still eat 17 percent of the world's timber.

We excrete an elephant's share of greenhouse gases. According to the most recent *US Statistical Abstract*, compiled by the Census Bureau, we throw away 232 million tons of garbage a year. In fact, Americans spend more on trash bags to get rid of our excess than ninety of the world's nations spend on everything they purchase — food, durable goods, health care — everything.

And how are we paying for all of this? Well, more than 40 percent of American families spend more money than they earn. The *Statistical Abstract* projects that in 2005, Americans will owe $985 billion on their credit cards alone. To keep up with our lifestyles, too many of us work too many hours, take a second mortgage on our homes, and still discover that we don't have enough.

We've already accumulated more stuff than anyone else on earth. Hooray for us! Are we the happiest nation on earth because of what we've been given? Is our faith stronger? Are we better adjusted, less fearful, more content?

No. Something is terribly wrong in America, and our staggering rates of obesity, depression, teen pregnancy, violence, and suicide are just symptoms of a larger problem.

Now I'm not a prophet in the traditional sense; God has not whispered into my ear and told me it's time for a revolution. But Jim Wallis argues that "Prophecy is not future telling, but articulating moral truth. The prophets diagnose the present and point the way to a just solution."[1] And if that's true, then, brother, wrap me in sackcloth and listen to me preach. I don't think we need a voice from heaven to tell us it's time we made a change in our priorities, pursued a different path. And one path that has had real meaning for me is what is known as voluntary simplicity.

People who practice voluntary simplicity make buying decisions based on what they truly need rather than what advertisers say they need. They replace the almighty dollar as the god of their daily lives with a life centered on family, friendship, and faith. In their buying choices, they try to live in harmony with the environment and with other people. And if they're anything like me, they try to reach the point where they don't buy things period, if they can help it. My friends the Barrons try to use Sunday as a Sabbath day from buying and selling, just as Orthodox Jews try not to touch money on their Sabbath, and I think it's a cool idea. What better way to demonstrate that we're not defined by what we buy than by refusing to buy anything?

I used to live the so-called American dream: a new house in suburbia, a new car, maxed-out credit cards. I had a whole lot of stuff, and a whole lot of unhappiness, even before I hit the skids with my depression.

But before I even knew what it was called, two experiences that I had at Baylor started me on the path to voluntary simplicity.

Ten years ago, in the summer of 1994, my good friend and Baylor colleague Blake Burleson took me as a faculty member on the Baylor in Africa program. It changed my life. For five weeks, I was part of a culture that disdained deadlines, treated distance as something better measured by stories than maps, and believed that "I" actually meant "we."

When we stayed with villagers in the hills of northwest Kenya, it was simultaneously the most challenging and the most illuminating experience of my life to that point. Some of our students went a little crazy, I think. Maybe I did too, because what I discovered seemed crazy to me. These members of the

Bukusu tribe, certainly among the world's poorest people, were some of the most joyful people I had ever met.

It made no sense. They possessed fewer clothes than I carried in my backpack, lived in crumbling houses of mud and wood, and cooked over open fires. I was raised to give my nickels and dimes to the Lottie Moon Christmas Fund for such people. But here was my new Bukusu friend Douglas Wanyama. He didn't have a library or a Palm Pilot or the complete second season of *The Sopranos*. But he had something better.

He had a smile on his face.

How could this be?

When you start asking questions, sometimes there's no stopping them. Each seemed to lead to another. Had stuff ever made me happy? No. Did the idea of pursuing more stuff make me happy? No. In fact, as I contemplated catalogs and shopping malls and credit card statements, it made me feel sad. Empty. The kind of feelings that make Americans want to go out and buy more stuff.

I think depression and consumption go hand in hand, and if buying something doesn't make you feel better, then maybe eating will, or drinking will.

In a nation full of depressed and alienated people, we are all trying to find the thing that will make us feel better, worthwhile, loved, but I am here to tell you that you cannot purchase it at Wal-Mart. It comes only as a gift, what Thomas Merton calls "the secret gift of happiness that God offers us," which we may not recognize because we insist "on a happiness that is approved by the magazines and TV" and "because we do not believe in a happiness that is given to us for nothing."[2]

"Free" is not the American way. But if we buy into the

American way, even if we call ourselves Christians or Jews or Muslims or Buddhists, then we are cutting ourselves off from real happiness, which never comes from a purchase but only from love and understanding. Thomas Moore wrote in a contemporary introduction to Merton that "care of the soul requires a high degree of resistance to the culture around us, simply because that culture is dedicated to values that have no concern for the soul. To preserve our precious hearts, we may have to live economically against the grain."[3]

I'm not saying these things because I hate America, so don't file me into a crank bin and decide you don't have to listen to me. I get the standard goose bumps singing "My Country, 'Tis of Thee," and I couldn't imagine living anywhere else. But I happen to believe it's disloyal to ask less of anything you love than it can be — your family, your church, your business, your nation. I'm saying this about the modern world in general and America in particular, because like people on both left and right, I think we have lost our moorings. We can call ourselves a Christian nation and even try to legislate a version of a Christian nation into being, but when we worship money, possessions, and the status we think they give us, we are turning our back on the hard teachings of Jesus about how we are supposed to live and love.

Jim Wallis has written about the "overwhelming focus on the poor in the Scriptures,"[4] and I've written elsewhere in this book about how those Scriptures that we sometimes push aside in our conception of Christianity call for justice and mercy and a real concern for the poor and oppressed. But, not surprisingly, the Scriptures also have things to say about wealth and acquisition, and mostly they're not positive.

Here is the merest sample:

"Consider the lilies of the field," Jesus said. "They toil not; neither do they sow. And yet even Solomon in all his glory was not arrayed as one of these."

"The love of money is the root of all evil," Paul said.

"I will not accept your gifts and offerings," the Hebrew prophet Amos said, speaking on behalf of God. "Not until you realize that being chosen is not a privilege; it is an obligation."

"Of those to whom much is given, much is expected," the Benedictine Rule tells us. (So does *Spider-Man*.)

But how much is expected? Well, maybe that question can be asked in this way: How much do I really need?

Every time I teach American literature, I use Henry David Thoreau's classic book *Walden* to introduce my class to the tensions between American values and American literature. But in fall 1994, just back from my first trip to Africa, I did not teach the book; the book taught me. Everything I had seen and learned in Africa, Thoreau was applying to life in bustling New England.

"What is truly necessary to life?" Thoreau asks in *Walden*. Our work and commerce, the hustle and hurry of our lives, the goods we lay up for ourselves, the mansions in which we shelter ourselves? No. "Simplicity, simplicity, simplicity," Thoreau advised, and at one point in the story, he actually throws his paperweight out the window as an object lesson.[5] Slow down. Reflect. Open your door and your heart to the natural world. Don't be afraid to march to the beat of a different drummer.

Even today, 150 years later, *Walden* is still a countercultural slap in the face of our consumer/information society, and even if you think you're right, I know it can be daunting to stand up and be counted.

"What do you want us to do?" some of my students invariably ask. "It's not like we can go off and live in a shack in the woods like Thoreau did."

"I know," I say. I'm not suggesting they do such a thing. Thoreau wasn't either. Like holy hermits throughout history, he was moving far enough away that his example could be seen and noted, but he wasn't calling for the entire world to move off the grid, and I have not given up my DVD player or my iPod.

Like Jesus, though, I think Thoreau was also offering up a parable from his life's example: A life lived in voluntary simplicity may be more fulfilling than a life lived according to society's standards. Better for you, better for those you love, better for the larger world.

I'll confess to you that in addition to Africa and Thoreau, divorce has also helped to teach me that life is not about possessions. Every time I've gone through separation and divorce, I've lost nearly everything, and I've had to come to terms with the idea that life had better not be about things, because things can disappear in the blink of an eye.

Don't lay up your riches on earth, Jesus said, where the fire can burn and the worm destroy—if your mom doesn't throw out your irreplaceable baseball cards when you go off to college, you'll probably lose them in the divorce settlement—but turn your sights toward heaven. And you don't have to turn your back on this world for the next to apply this message; what Jesus meant was that spiritual things matter, and that only they last. The world may tell you that you have to have the biggest SUV, the biggest house, the biggest whatever. But as Don Henley says in one of his songs, "You don't see no hearses with luggage racks."

Perhaps you're starting to see how a simpler life might be better for you and your family. But how is it better for the larger world, you might ask. What possible difference do my decisions make?

A lot more than you know. As an example, in the last ten years, news sources from the *Los Angeles Times* to *Reuters* to the Christian social justice magazine *The Other Side* have all chronicled the labor practices of contractors making products for Disney, the American icon described by the National Labor Committee as one of the "greediest sweat shop abusers" in the world.[6] You've probably never given it any thought, but did you know that the item of Disney apparel you're taking to the check-out stand may have been made by a woman in a sweatshop in Bangladesh who was beaten and threatened during her fifteen-hour work shift? That she earned a nickel in wages for that shirt for which you're about to pay $40?

Can you see how, in the process of making even this simple choice to buy a popular logo, ordinary Americans like you and me have become unwitting supporters of oppression and injustice?

Probably not. These aren't stories we often hear from the main-stream media, most of whom are owned by huge multinational conglomerates who exist to sell us stuff. They aren't stories we even want to hear. But it is, nonetheless, an important part of the concept of voluntary simplicity. Voluntary simplicity is not just about giving things up that you don't need. It's about spending less when you do buy, about reducing, reusing, and recycling to walk more lightly on the planet we share with the other 95 percent of human beings. It also has to do with recognizing that today our simplest consumer choices may have a moral dimension.

It takes effort to be a conscious consumer, because it means you have to be a well-informed consumer. It means knowing what stores offer sweatshop merchandise to us because we are so addicted to the low, low price. It means researching how stores compensate their workers, if they provide health insurance or rely on the state to take care of their poor associates, how much those businesses give back to the community. For example, I would never own a Windows-based computer because I've been a Mac user all my life; but all the same, I have to admire the Microsoft record of responsibility to its workers and the incredible generosity of its founders, who have given billions of dollars back to the world instead of holding onto it like some of the filthiest rich. If Microsoft could make a decent operating system, I wouldn't feel at all guilty about using it.

Now, if you're like me, the thought of morally examining your purchase of a pair of socks may be enough to make you slap your hands to your face and scream like Macaulay Culkin in the movie *Home Alone*. But don't despair. It is still, as that quintessential American capitalist Benjamin Franklin once said, possible to do well *and* do good. There are easy choices you can make that might cost a little more, but will make you and the world feel a whole lot better.

By buying fair-trade coffee, for example, you can be assured that coffee pickers in Latin America are paid a living wage for their labor. By refusing to patronize the many megastores selling goods made with child or sweatshop labor, you can send a message to retailers that you aren't willing to sacrifice women and children on the altar of convenience. By shopping in a thrift or consignment store or buying a used car, you can save money and natural resources. Even through something as simple as paying a little more for organic produce you can keep pesticides and chemical fertilizers off your food, out of our water, and away from the workers who picked that produce.

Sometimes people ask me why I live the way I do. Unlike other longtime professors at Baylor, I don't wear suits and drive a new car and live in a nice house. I am fairly compensated for the work that I do, and perhaps they wonder why when I lived in Waco I rode my bike to school every day instead of driving, why now I drive an old car and live in an efficiency apartment. Some of them, I think, find it a little shameful, as though my adopted poverty reflects badly on them.

Although I have at times been awfully poor, post-divorce, the fact is, I could afford a little better. It is less a logistical issue now than a moral one. The truth of the matter is, now I am like Douglas, my friend from Kenya, poor but happy. In fact, now that I know what happiness feels like, I can tell you that I am happiest when I pursue what Henri Nouwen cleverly called "downward mobility," seeking to serve instead of seeking reward.

It turns out that the whole losing yourself to find yourself thing does eventually pay off big. Owning things didn't give me joy, the love of my friends and family does. And although I don't have a lot of money, I am content to spend what I must in the wisest way possible — making good choices and buying only what I need — and to give what I can away.

I use the library instead of buying new books that I would read once and then park on a shelf. I'm happy to take my kids to the public pool at the seminary where they can be in community instead of having a big fenced backyard and my own private pool. I go to a lot of free events in Austin where we watch movies or listen to music under the stars. I ride my bike. If my car breaks down, I ride the bus.

My life is finally not about what I earn and what I spend, but what I get and what I give, and even before I got well, I was starting to understand this.

So, simplicity can help bond friends and family. Sustainable living can help us treat our resources with respect so this planet can welcome our children and their children. A life focused on family, God, and community is rich in delight. And voluntary simplicity can be an important part of a spiritual practice: This is God's wealth. I try to keep only what I truly need and give the rest away.

I do not want to be an elephant.

It may be a disturbing thing to discover that there are people beneath our feet; it certainly was for me when I began to understand that my money was supporting injustice. But I'm encouraged beyond measure by this: With patience and concentration, even elephants can learn to walk more lightly.

charity

Though there may be times when your hands are empty,
your heart is always full, and you can give things out of that.

FRANCES HODGSON BURNETT, *A LITTLE PRINCESS*

It was the eighth day of Christmas, and you had better believe that if I had a true love somewhere, she hadn't given me anything. The calendar had just turned over to January 2002, and although we were only a few days into the month, I had already spent everything I had. My guitar and amplifier were in the pawnshop, and it was only days until I lost them. The transmission had fallen out of my car a few weeks before, and although Tinamarie was letting me use her old Volvo sedan to haul Jake and Chandler around Austin, school started in two weeks, and when it did, I had no way to drive the 100 miles to work.

It was true that I had two checks coming from writing gigs I'd finished, but I had been expecting one for weeks and the other for months, and I wasn't rushing to check the mail anymore. Bills get airlifted to your mailbox; the checks seem to take some kind of banana boat by way of Guatemala.

The point, really, is this: Two days into the month I was out of money, and I knew this because my four-year-old son Chandler and I had just driven Tinamarie's car up to the post office and mailed off my paycheck in pieces to my creditors, while my teenage son Jake waited back at my apartment for us to return.

The night was cold and dark, and the wind cut through my clothes as Chandler and I walked back to the car. A shape moved out of the darkness to stand next to the rear bumper — a small black woman in a navy blue hooded sweatshirt. She could have been forty; she could have been sixty.

She was shivering.

"Can you help me please?" she asked. It's the same thing I have heard — you have heard — everywhere, the world over. I've been panhandled in New York and New Orleans and Nairobi. And when I hear it, or something like it, my answer is almost always, "I'm sorry."

Which is what I told this woman on this night, stepping forward a bit to put myself between her and Chandler. She was not an imposing figure, but she had stepped out of the darkness, and he was a little frightened.

Now, I know the Homeless Polka. I say "I'm sorry," and they're supposed to say something like "Okay, God bless you."

You put your left foot in. You put your left foot out.

But this woman didn't know the steps. She didn't move from the back of the car.

No — she stepped closer.

She stepped closer, and she looked me in the eye, and she said, "Please. I haven't eaten for two days. I'm cold. Can't you give me ten dollars?"

And I believed that she was hungry, and I believed that she was cold. I could hear it in her voice.

I could see it in her eyes.

But what I said again was "I'm sorry," a little more forcefully this time. "I can't help you." Chandler was huddled behind me, holding on to my leg, and I dropped a hand for him to hold.

"Please," she said. "Please. Just ten dollars."

I shook my head. I opened the back door and lifted Chandler inside, out of the cold, keeping one eye on her. I didn't know what to make of things. She should have been walking away. But she wasn't. As I belted him in his car seat, I could see her through the side window, no more than three feet away.

She was crying when I finished with Chandler and straightened back up, her face contorted. "Please," she said. "Can't you give me something? Anything?"

I had eighteen dollars in my wallet, all I had left from my paycheck. I didn't know where the next eighteen was coming from. All I knew was that I didn't know how I was going to buy groceries until my next paycheck, and I was getting ready to lose my guitar and my amp, and if I couldn't get a car to get to school, I was going to lose my job.

I looked at her, at her crumpled face, at her tears. I looked at her and I said, just barely controlling my anger, "Go away. You're scaring my child. I can't help you."

And she just stood there, looking at me, like maybe she didn't understand me, or maybe she didn't want to, so I kept talking. "I can't help you. I can't even take care of my kids. Don't ask me for help."

I was, even in those days, trying to be a Christian. I teach compassion and justice. I wanted to help her.

But I closed Chandler's door, and then shaking my head, I got into the car and turned the key.

As the engine started, she ran off for the far end of the parking lot. I could hear her calling to a man getting into a Mercedes. I did not stay long enough to see if she reached him, if he stopped to listen. I backed up, and then we lurched out into the street.

"Why did that person want money?" Chandler asked in his tiny mouse's voice as we headed down Sixth Street on our way home.

I thought for a moment before I answered. "She said that she was hungry," I told him. "She said she was cold."

"But we don't have any money," he said.

"I know," I said.

I turned right onto Lamar, and we drove in silence for a bit, both of us thinking.

"Are we going to tell Jacob about that person?" he asked.

"Do you want to?" I asked.

"Yes," he said.

"Okay," I said.

He ran up the sidewalk to my apartment and threw the door open. "A person at the post office was hungry," Chandler breathlessly announced as soon as we were inside.

Jake put a finger in his book and arched his eyebrow at me for a translation.

"A homeless woman asked me for money at the post office," I said quietly.

Jake is a Joan Baez soul in a Shaquille O'Neal body. He has size fourteen shoes and a size fourteen heart. He looked at my face and said, "Dad, you can't help everyone."

"I know," I said. Chandler had started shrugging off his clothes right there in the living room, so I sent him back to get ready for his bath.

"You help people," Jake went on. "All the time."

"Yes," I said. I sat down heavily on the arm of the couch. "People." I looked down at the floor. "But this was a person."

He nodded and opened his book. I bit my lip, got up, and went back to run the water for Chandler's bath. The warm water felt good on my hand after the cold walk from the car, and it felt good to be in for the evening. After Chandler climbed into the bath, I started emptying my pockets onto the bathroom counter.

I opened my wallet, pulled out the bills and laid them down on the counter, one by one: a ten, a five, three ones. About sixty cents in change. Five Fender medium guitar picks, in case my ship came in and my guitar came home.

Chandler had the beginnings of an eye infection, and since Tinamarie had gone out of town for a day or two, I was doctor on duty. I decided to wash his face carefully with soap, although this idea did not meet with his favor.

"Keep your eyes closed," I told him.

"Will it hurt?" he kept asking.

"I'll do my best," is what I said.

When we were done, when I had rinsed all the soap from his face, I asked him to open his eyes. He did it slowly, in stages, like someone emerging from a dark cave into the light.

"It didn't hurt," he said to me in wonder.

"No," I said.

"Why not?" he asked. He asked why about everything in those days. Why did Stevie Ray Vaughn die? Why isn't Grandpa

Jerry my daddy? Why do they call it a refrigerator? Why didn't I get soap in my eyes?

"Because I washed your face very carefully," I told him. "Because I washed it with love." I was pretty proud of myself.

"Oh," he said. "Okay. I want to play now."

"Okay," I said. I got up and closed the curtain so he could splash.

And as I rose, I saw the ten dollar bill sitting on the corner.

Now, I have never been the kind of Christian who believes that giving your money away is the ticket to prosperity. I do not believe in a God who offers you a return on your investments.

What I believed in, even then, was a Messiah who said, "I was hungry and you fed me. I was naked, and you clothed me," a God who wants us to make a difference in the world, regardless of the cost.

And so I was ashamed. I knew that what I had done was rational, logical, that I was cash poor, that my income stream did not indicate a move toward philanthropy at the present time.

But I was ashamed just the same.

It's fortunate that I also believe in a God of the second chance, a Savior who could look past his own suffering to say to a dying but repentant thief, "Today you will be with me in Paradise," a God who believes it is never too late to wake up from sleep and do the right thing.

So I called Jake into the bathroom. "Can you watch Chandler for a few minutes?" I asked.

"Sure," he said. And although I think he knew exactly what I was doing, he asked, "Where are you going?"

"I'll be back in fifteen minutes," I said, stuffed the ten into my pocket, and went back out into the cold.

Maybe you think you know the happy ending to my story. I certainly thought I did. As I drove back down to the post office, I was already seeing it in my head, how I would give her the money, how I would tell her I would pray for her, how I would ask her to pray for me, a PhD one paycheck from the pavement himself.

But the vast parking lot was empty. I got out and checked the alcoves of the building, I checked the stairs leading down to Fifth Street, I checked under the stairs. I went back and sat on my trunk for a few minutes, shivering, thinking that she still might magically appear.

But, of course, she did not. I saw a figure disappear into an alley across the street, and I breathed a prayer for that person, whoever it was.

I breathed a prayer that the man in the Mercedes had been more generous than me.

And then I went home to my boys. Chandler was out of the bath, warm and pink and ready for bed. Both of them looked up at me inquisitively as I walked in, and I shook my head.

"She was gone," I said.

"Why?" Chandler asked.

"Maybe somebody else helped her," I said. But I didn't really believe that.

I sat again on the arm of the couch. "You guys sit down," I directed, and they did, side by side, mammoth teenager, dainty little four-year-old.

"I think," I said, speaking slowly and carefully, "that I made a mistake tonight." ("Mistake" was a word Tinamarie and I had used with Chandler.) "I thought I knew better than this. But tonight I chose not to help someone who needed help. Tonight I chose to think about myself. I think that—for me—that was the wrong choice. It's not the example I want to set for you. I'm sorry."

Jake started to say, "But at least you went back—" and I raised my hand.

"You don't have to make me feel better," I said. "I think it's okay if I just feel sad for a while."

"Okay," he said. And so I did.

On my second trip to the post office, I had imagined how it would feel to give her that ten, how my heart would have been lifted, how I would have known that I was doing the right thing.

I did—I do—believe in a God of second chances. But I also believe that sometimes we only have one chance to do the right thing, and if we don't take it, the situation shifts and that chance is gone forever. I thought I had learned this lesson, that my eyes were open, but when the trial came, I was tired and I was cold and I was afraid, and I did the wrong thing.

But maybe next time the lesson will stick, and I will do something different. Maybe I will *be* different. Maybe my boys will be different. Or maybe you will.

Dr. King used to say, "The time is always right to do what is right." And what he meant by that and what I mean by that are the same thing, I think. We have to pursue social justice if we ever want to have a truly just society. But I want to take it a step further, as I know Dr. King also did. Like him, I believe we are called to act as Christ's hands, to help others. I believe that doing the right thing is much much much more important than not doing what some folks say is the wrong thing. It may in fact be the only important thing.

And I believe that maybe it is our fear, and only our fear, that has kept us from hearing all those radical gospel messages, that keeps Jesus from truly being let loose in the world.

CONFIRMATION

sin

I do buy the idea that we are flawed,
that there is something in us that is broken.
I think it is easier to do bad things than good things.

DONALD MILLER, *BLUE LIKE JAZZ*

Okay, here's a story I really don't want to tell you. And I mean that for lots of reasons, only one of which is that this story is tremendously embarrassing and makes me look really bad. It makes me look bad, because it not only depicts me doing bad things but thinking about doing yet other bad things. And if you've been reading along so far and imagining that I'm a pretty nice guy, the kind you might like to introduce to your neighbors, I'm afraid that at the end of it you'll have seen the real me, or at least as much of the real me as I'm willing for you and the people I work with and the parishioners who might someday employ me to see, and that you won't look at me the same after that.

But it's also a good story, and I am a slave to good stories, especially when they end well.

It's a story about sin, about my top-of-the-charts most shameful moment, and although you could poll people who know me well who might say that I've done worse, things that hurt them more, this is the moment I am most ashamed of as I look back over the years I'm chronicling in this book, and maybe over my entire life.

And that is why I need to tell you about it, because I want you to know that even a serious Christian like me has done bad things, and I want you to know that, even though I'm not one of those Christians who hands out salvation tracts on street corners, I know that there is such a thing as sin.

Here's what I think about sin: I think, first, that it's not necessarily the things we usually think of when we hear the word, like looking at nekkid women or playing the lottery. I start with Thomas Merton's definition, that sin is "inequality, injustice, which seeks more for myself than my rights allow and which gives others less than they should receive. To love myself more than others is to be untrue to myself as well as to them."[1] Although it is the way of the world and certainly is our nature, selfishness — putting myself first — leads to separation from others, from our essential selves, and separation from God and what God wants for us, whatever that might be.

So selfishness is sin, and sin is selfishness.

Where does depression fit in? Depression is a tricky thing to talk about, because it's biochemical, hereditary, can be caused by diet or accident or situation, and I don't want in any way to infer that depression is a sinful condition. But it is a selfish condition. My poet friend Martha, when I went to visit her once in New Haven at Yale Divinity School, was in the deepest blue depths of a blue patch while I was with her, and since I was just in my hazy gray unhappy days back then, I couldn't yet comprehend her deep unhappiness. "Depression is totally selfish," she told me one cold dark Connecticut night. "It's like you're all there is. There's no one else."

And what I think she meant by that, if my later experience is any guide, is that when you're suffering from serious depression, your own unhappiness is the dark filter through which everything flows. If someone else is joyful, that joy turns to crap flung in your face when it goes through the filter. If someone else is hurting, that pain somehow turns to personal pain. And so on, and so forth. I remember that in a lucid moment, I wrote in my journal, "I'm so sick of all this me me me me. I'm just not that important. Why can't I think about something else?"

But I couldn't. I was drowning in myself and in my unhappiness, and it was a closed system, like the terrarium my mom helped me build when I was a little kid, unhappiness creating more unhappiness.

So let me be absolutely clear—although I think people who are depressed may hurt others and themselves because of their depression, I do not consider depression to be sin. I do not agree with my family members who felt that if I prayed a little harder, I'd get better, or who suggested that if I ordered Satan out of my apartment, the sky would clear. I do think that depression has a spiritual as well as an emotional and physical component, because a major part of my cure was spiritual, but I also know that there are devout people of faith who continue to suffer depression despite their love of God.

I can't tell you why I got better and other people didn't, why I lived and other people died. All I can tell you is that I finally came to a point where I could see that there was more to the world than the black hole of my despair, and God and God's loving people were the reason.

But until that moment, although I could escape that black hole for a while to do my work or love my sons, it was only temporary, often very temporary, and eventually my orbit would take me down, down, like something orbiting the inside of the toilet bowl on the way to wherever plumbing goes. My moments of competence were real, but costly; after I rocked an hour-long class, I usually came back to my office, locked the door, turned out the lights, and curled up in my office recliner to try and hold it all together.

In those days, I spent an awful lot of time in the dark.

When Tinamarie invited me to her thirtieth birthday party in October 2001, we had been split for a year, but I still wasn't handling it well. My first questions were, "Will X be there? And will Y be there?"

Actually, she had quit seeing Y, who was also an acquaintance of mine, and who left a mournful message on my machine the day of the party telling me he wasn't going and that I should go and enjoy myself.

"I've invited all my friends," she said, which was the last thing I wanted to hear, because not only did that include X and Y (and Z, as it turned out), it meant that this was going to be a huge gathering of her cool, artsy, gentle-on-the-earth, granola friends where I would be the only person with a 9-to-5 job, and the only ex-husband of the birthday girl.

"I'm not coming," I told her, which sent her immediately into a bad place. Her family considers birthdays and holidays only slightly less important occasions than I imagine V-E Day was, and for me not to come was going to rain on her parade. Birthdays and holidays had to be exactly right. Still do, actually.

Well, what could I do? We were still friends, we were raising a child together, and if the truth were known, in those days I still desperately wanted her back. I thought maybe if I did this and was nice and charming and debonair — I was thinking Cary Grant, or at least Hugh Grant — maybe this nightmare could still have a happy ending.

And besides, she went on, Chandler wanted me to come, and she needed me to watch him.

"I'll watch him," I said. "Over here." My apartment was about five blocks away from Tinamarie and Chandler's, a detail which was convenient then and proves important later.

"If you watch him there, then he won't be able to come to the party," she said, "and he wants to come to the party."

Well, it had a certain logic.

Tinamarie had often invited me to gatherings of her family of friends, who were artists and musicians and otherwise creative and free, but although I was also an artist and a musician, I never felt comfortable around them.

Truth be told, I resented them. In some twisted way, instead of recognizing that Tinamarie left me because I had been a horribly mean and untrustworthy person in the years after Chandler was born, I chose to think that somehow she had left me for them, traded me in on a newer model with a nicer stereo and better mileage. I also felt dreadfully uncool around them because I had a day job and health insurance, and although I now understand that that's actually pretty cool in a country where forty million people don't have health insurance and need it, my never-high self-esteem had not been improved by depression, separation, and loneliness.

So when I was around Tinamarie's friends, which was as

rarely as I could manage, I was even more introverted than usual, and I doubt if they liked me any better than I liked them, because I'd given them little reason to. Of them all, only our mutual friend, Raj — and how he managed to walk that tightrope, I don't know — was as much mine as hers.

"I don't want to come," I told her, which does not mean the same thing as "I won't," and she knew it. Part of me told myself that I was being selfish, and as I said, I consider that to be sinful. Hurting someone else is a bad thing.

But then again, so is hurting yourself.

Conundrum.

So that's where we left it, with her expecting me to come, and me not sure I'd agreed to and hoping I hadn't, but knowing I probably would.

In those days, I was having these horrible free-floating anxiety attacks — I'd lie in bed some nights, my heart pounding, afraid of God knows what. The future. The present. Being broke. Being alone for the rest of my life. Everything and nothing.

Now I had something concrete for my anxiety to light on: a big party.

You will have figured out by now that I'm a shy person, and so it won't surprise you to hear that I don't like large parties. Any large parties. I would have been miserable if they had been sixty of my closest friends. I would have been looking for the nearest bathroom to lock myself in, the nearest potted plant to hide behind. And a gathering with my ex-wife and one or more of her past or present boyfriends, and a bunch of people who I don't know, and a bunch of other people I know but don't like —

Well, maybe that will help you find some forgiveness for me when I tell you that I began drinking in the early afternoon and, by the time of Tinamarie's birthday party, was what I would have to call working on tomorrow's serious hangover.

Now, I don't advocate alcohol as a social leveler or a coping mechanism, and I think it was a really bad idea that night — my story, in fact, proves it — but I can also tell you that I felt trapped and miserable and couldn't imagine even walking into that gathering until I had a six-pack under my belt, when at least I could imagine it.

I wouldn't have described myself as having a drinking problem in those days — I didn't drink every day, or even every week, and I didn't drive to Tinamarie's party — but I can think of situations when I drank to avoid or to numb or to get through something, all of which are pretty good functional definitions for a drinking problem. So you make the call.

I walked over to the party, which was being held in the open space between houses owned by some of her friends and her apartment and the house where Z lived. As I went up on the back porch where the drinks were, I suddenly found myself within twelve inches of X, and in that moment, I had an almost uncontrollable urge to throw his skinny gentle self down the stairs.

Now I am not a violent person, although I have told you that I had more than too much badly expressed anger in my marriage to Tinamarie and in the years just after. I'm actually a pacifist, and unless you're threatening my family, you can be pretty sure that you're safe around me. In theory, I can't justify violence, and I think it's unChristian.

But I had had too much to drink, and I couldn't stand the thought of Tinamarie being with this pinhead instead of me, and I swear to you, it is only by the grace of God that I didn't hurt him badly.

I was shaking, and my hands were trembling I hated him so. I'm sure he could feel it, because he eased greasily away from me like his feet were melting underneath him.

It was at that point that I made my way through the crowd to find Tinamarie, because I knew at that moment I should not be there. When I found her, she hugged me and started to introduce me to five more of her granola people, and I pulled her aside.

"I have to go," I told her.

"Have you been drinking?" she asked me. I don't know if it was the smell or my behavior or a secret power that women have.

"Yes," I said. I may have said, "I've had a few," because that was my answer for Tinamarie in those days when she asked, whether I'd had two or twelve. But I honestly don't remember, because I was too drunk.

"Chandler's looking for you," she said, and I think I told her again, "I can't be here," and she blew it off, and clearly both of us made a mistake in not listening to me.

So I must have been watching Chandler, or seeing multiple Chandlers, although again, I don't remember clearly. At one point, Raj told me he needed to go to the place where he was staying, a couple of blocks away, and I seized on him like the drowning man I was.

"I'll be back in a bit," I told Tinamarie, who looked miffed at suddenly having Chandler duty in the middle of her birthday bash but didn't say it, and off I went, and I stayed gone for a good long time.

I knew it was too long, and I also knew I didn't want to go back, and felt put upon that I would have to, and so, drunk and angry and depressed and self-conscious, I at last walked back toward Tinamarie's birthday party, and there she was, standing in the middle of the street with Chandler in her arms, waiting for me.

I'm sure she asked me where I'd been, but again things are such a mixed-up mess of images, that all I really remember is this: I threw a fit. All that tamped-down anger came out, and not just out there in the middle of the street. After I'd yelled and screamed and generally scared my four-year-old half to death, I walked back into the party to scream at Tinamarie some more. And there, surrounded by all the cool kids, I showed the world who I really was: A brute. A drunk. An angry and sad and hopeless man.

And when I was done, Tinamarie told me that I had ruined her birthday, and since I pretty much had to agree that having your drunk ex-husband scream curses at you in the middle of your birthday party has to rank right up there toward the top in horrible ways to celebrate, I went home with a boulder-sized guilt weighing me down.

There are no words to explain how horrible I felt at that moment, how hopeless, how stained. I knew that I would apologize later, and that I should apologize, and that nothing I did could ever erase the harm I had done, the pain I'd caused, the shame I felt.

That was the way I always felt in those days when I'd hurt Tinamarie and scared Chandler, it was what had propelled me down the street to almost end my life in Santa Fe, and when I got home to my tiny apartment, I sat on the floor in the dark and shook. Shuddered, maybe, would be a better word. Shivered.

I shook because I was having that feeling again, that feeling that really I'd be so much better off dead, that everybody would be better off, that I didn't want to ever hurt anybody again, I didn't want to be hurt again, I didn't want to be lost or lonely or out of control, and I only knew one way to make that happen.

I had almost a whole bottle of sleeping pills in my cabinet. I had counted them another dark night, dreamily, like you might imagine Scrooge McDuck counting money. I didn't take them anymore because they were addictive, because, in fact, I had discovered that I couldn't sleep unless I took them, and I had just stopped taking them, quietly, without telling anyone why I was sweating and shaking and throwing up for days on end.

But I kept them, even though I didn't take them for my insomnia anymore.

I kept them because there were a lot of them, and because I didn't have a gun, and because who knew if a car wreck would kill me.

Just to be safe, you understand.

So I was shaking because I really wanted to kill myself, and I thought I had solved this problem once already, and if I hadn't solved it, would I ever, short of death, and because Tinamarie and Chandler must hate me, and even Raj was probably disgusted with me, because I was disgusted with me, and because I was all alone, again, like that old Gilbert O'Sullivan song "Alone Again (Naturally)," which ends, I think, with the guy throwing himself off something tall.

Then my fingers brushed across the phone, and suddenly I was dialing, and miracle of miracles, the ringing stopped and Chris said, in his calm and loving voice, "What's going on, Buddy?"

"I'm afraid I'm going to do something bad to myself," I

told him and explained why, and I was ashamed all over again, having to tell my best friend what a terrible person I was.

But he didn't judge, and he didn't scold. He listened. And he loved.

He stayed on the phone with me until I could tell him that I didn't think I was a danger to myself anymore, which took a long time.

What Chris was for me that night was the voice of God letting me know that no matter what I'd done, I was still loved. I was still valuable. That, impossible as it was to imagine, there was still something worth living for, a plan I hadn't even seen the contours of yet.

Anne Lamott reminds us that God is like an adoptive parent who chooses not only the good-looking kid at the orphanage, one of whose parents might have been a Nobel Prize-winning chemist, but also the mongrel kid, the mean kid, the crack baby with the congenital heart defect. "So of course he loves old ordinary me," she says, "even or especially at my most scared and petty and mean and obsessive. Loves me; *chooses* me."[2]

If Chris hadn't picked up the phone that night, if I hadn't had someone tell me that I was still loved and chosen, then it's entirely possible that I would not have awakened the next morning with a splitting headache and the realization that I had a whole lot o' 'splainin' to do. I doubt, in fact, that I would ever have awakened again.

But I did, and although it was awful, I apologized to Tinamarie and to Chandler. I apologized to God. I'm sorry, I told them all. I can do better. I don't know why this is all so hard for me.

It was the apostle Paul who also said that he didn't know why he had so much trouble with sin. He knew what he ought to be doing, but sure enough, when push came to shove, he'd do the thing he knew he shouldn't.

Maybe I should never have gone to Tinamarie's birthday party. I'm willing to entertain that notion. But if I was going to go, certainly I should have had enough respect not to show up drunk, or to want to do violence to her guests, or to run away and hide when I'd said I'd watch over Chandler, or to scream at her. Twice. All of the things I did, even if I might have thought I was doing them out of self-preservation, were selfish things, things in which I was thinking only of myself.

I know that I have done worse things to Tinamarie and to Chandler. But not so many different kinds of selfish things in so little time, and not in front of such a large audience.

Someday I hope to look back on this and laugh; I can't now, not yet. Even though Tinamarie has forgiven me and Chandler has forgotten it, I haven't forgotten. And although I don't beat myself up over it, it scares me to know that the mean drunk is a person I could have become, not just that one time, but forever.

When I was sunk in depression and racked with insomnia, I was also sunk in myself, to the exclusion of everybody else's pain and suffering. Sometimes it seemed almost impossible to do anything but bad things. And for that reason — although I say again, for the third time, that depression does not equal sin — I have to say that I'm thankful that I can think about other people again. That I can consider somebody else's pain before my own. That I finally flew out of that black hole and into a bright corner of the universe.

This story is a confession of sorts, that I have sinned in thought, word, and deed, that I have not loved my neighbor as myself. At St. James we confess our sins at every Eucharist — not like I just did, in mind-numbing detail, but still — and when we're done, we sit there for a moment, lost in our selves, lost in our sin as Greg gets up from his knees. Then he stands, and he raises his right hand, and he blesses us.

"Almighty God have mercy on you," he says, making the sign of the cross over us, "forgive you all your sins through our Lord Jesus Christ, strengthen you in all goodness, and by the power of the Holy Spirit, keep you in eternal life."

"Amen," we say, and that's also what I feel. I've sinned all my life — or what I thought was sin, because I certainly felt guilty enough for looking at nekkid women — but in the church where I grew up, although we talked about forgiveness, we never got any. Every Sunday, now, I confess that I've put myself first and that I want to do better, and every Sunday, I hear the voice of God saying that whatever I've done, I'm still loved. I'm still valuable. That there's still a plan for me.

One of my favorite old hymns is called "Love Lifted Me," and it's about how I was sunk in sin and love pulled me out, like a sailor with a gaff hook. We rarely sing that hymn at St. James, but still, that's how I feel every time Greg brings us those words of absolution: Rescued. Strengthened in goodness.

Chosen.

And ready for whatever comes next.

neighbors

I like to think that I'm a compassionate person, that I'm not prejudiced or biased against people based on who they are or what they look like or what they believe.

I like to think that, but I have to tell you that it's not totally true.

I used to have a feeble joke — I don't tell good jokes; all my humor is situational, as you may have noticed — anyway, I used to say, "I'm intolerant of intolerant people," and by that, what I really meant was that I didn't like people who didn't like the same things I liked.

Because although racism has been a lifelong issue for me and I try never to judge a person by the color of his or her skin, I'm still likely to be prejudiced against people who shop in Wal-Mart, or patchouli-smelling dancers and candle makers and other such folk who do not shave any part of their bodies and who follow their bliss in ways that I would never dare to.

So, hooray for me.

If you're black or brown or bronze, I'll go out of my way to be nice to you.

Unless, of course, you're headed into a Wal-Mart. And then, you better watch out.

Throughout the Hebrew Scriptures, the Jews were told that they needed to extend justice to those less fortunate, to widows and the poor and to the resident alien, but the concept of who, exactly, you were supposed to be kind to gets reflected in some questions that Jesus fields in the tenth chapter of the gospel of Luke. When a student of the laws — a lawyer, he's called in many translations, but he wasn't the kind of guy who could draw up your will or sue you for your last shekel — when this lawyer asks Jesus what he needs to do to be holy, Jesus gives him an answer that appears in several of the Gospels: the heart of the law is to love God entirely and to love your neighbor as yourself.

"Ah," the lawyer says, seeing his wiggle room. "But who, exactly, *is* my neighbor?"

In other words, he's asking, do I have to love the people near me, the people like me, the people I run into in the course of a normal day? Because that, maybe, I can do.

Maybe.

He wanted an easy answer, but Jesus didn't give him one. Instead, as he often does in the Gospels, he told a story, which went something like this:

Lo, there was a man who went down the road from Jerusalem to Jericho. Along the way, he was ambushed by thieves, who stripped him of everything he had and left him for dead by the side of the road. Now, a priest came down the road, and when he saw him, he passed over to the other side and left him there. And then a Levite, a holy man, saw him, and he also passed him by.

But a Samaritan of a nation hated by the Jews saw him lying there and was moved with pity, and he bound the man's wounds as best he could and carried him on his donkey to an inn for the night. The next morning, he paid the innkeeper to take care of the injured man until he was well and told him, "Whatever it costs, I'll repay you when I see you again."

Then Jesus looked at the lawyer and asked his own question: "Of the three who passed by the wounded man, which one was his neighbor?"

I don't know if the lawyer was chastened or chagrined, but the storyteller in me likes to think he was simply moved by the truth of Jesus' story, the wisdom of Jesus himself, and that he answered quietly, "The one who showed him mercy."

At that Jesus nodded, seeing he had made his point, and said, gently, "Then go and do the same."

The Good Samaritan has always been one of my favorite parables, which is what the teaching stories of Jesus are called. First, it's about race and intolerance — a Samaritan was the last person you'd expect to stop and help a Jew, because the Jew probably would not have stopped to help the Samaritan if their situations had been reversed. Second, it talks about putting love into action, which I keep telling you is what Christianity is all about. And third, this story is one of the models for stories of superheroes, which, as you may know, I really like. Spider-Man doesn't just save Aunt May; he saves everyone who needs rescuing.

It's also a story that keeps slapping me in the face, in the way that things you need to learn keep putting themselves in your way. Anne Lamott has written about a little problem she had forgiving a certain person, and how all of a sudden God became like Sam I Am from Dr. Seuss's *Green Eggs and Ham*, appearing out of every nook and cranny with helpful hints about forgiveness.[1]

As I've said, I'm a tolerant person who happens to have a little problem with tolerance. And it's easy enough to forget that I have this problem, because, like most of us, I tend not to go places where there are people radically different from me in belief, outlook, or shopping habits, so it's easy for me to think I'm a paragon of openness.

Which is where the divine Sam I Am comes in.

I drive ancient Volvos. Since we moved to Austin in 2000, I've bought five of them, I think. Three of them were station wagons, which were great because they had room for my amp, guitar, stands, and the like, plus when I went camping, if I didn't want to put up my tent I could just push down the backseat and spread out my sleeping bag. My favorite Volvo to date was a 1983 maroon station wagon that I drove all over these United States, from Colorado to North Carolina, doing book appearances and playing music when *Free Bird* came out in 2002.

Now the nice thing about owning an ancient Volvo is you don't have to make payments on it. The less nice thing is that although they will run forever if you take care of them, they are ancient, and things can go wrong, stop working, or fall off that will have to be fixed. In fact, I wrote a blues song that I still perform occasionally called "AM Radio," which is a catalog of things that might go wrong with an ancient car, ending with the worst, that finally the only thing you will be able pick up over your speakers will be hate radio and Spanish-language evangelists in Monterey.

If you drive an ancient car over long distances, eventually something essential will fail and you will be stranded. This is, I think, one of the five monumental scientific theorems that Albert Einstein proved in 1905.

Since ancient cars do break down and I was driving thousands and thousands of miles in one, I finally bought a cell phone in 2002, both so I could stay in touch on the road and so I could call for help. But since, as I mentioned, God wanted me to learn some things, my maroon Volvo almost always broke down in places where I had no cell phone coverage, where I couldn't rely on my own resources.

In the summer of 2003 I'd had a writing residency to finish the first draft of my novel *Sanctuary* at Ghost Ranch, up in northern New Mexico, and it had gone really well. On the way home in August, when the rear right tire blew out sixty miles north of Roswell, New Mexico, I wasn't too worried.

I pulled onto the shoulder of US 285, jacked up the car, and put on my spare.

And then, one mile down the road, when my spare went flat, I pulled out my cell phone.

"No Service," it said, and I began to panic.

Okay, panic may be too strong a word. I was in the wellness zone by then, and although I didn't know how this was going to work out, I figured something would happen to help me. I just didn't know what.

I hoisted the first flat out of the back of the wagon — it was very heavy, and the inner rim of the wheel cut into the fingers on my left hand — and started walking south, along the side of the highway. When I heard a car coming, I would turn and lift a thumb, just as I'd seen it done in movies, and then I turned and started walking again as new SUV after new SUV swooshed past and left me standing.

Then a tiny car — something like a Chevy Cavalier but with only two doors — pulled over and began to back toward me. As it approached, I couldn't even see the driver for the stuff piled in the backseat; my view was blocked by an ice chest and an economy-size bag of chips. When the car came even with me, the passenger door swung open, and a largish woman piled out.

"You get on in here," she said to me.

She put her seat forward and somehow rearranged the things in the backseat so she could wedge my flat on top and push the seat back. Then she scooted over, straddling the console, and said again, "Get on in here."

I may have mentioned that I'm kind of a shy person, but let me say that there was no way to be shy inside a tiny car filled to bursting with stuff and carrying me and two largish people, one of whom was partly sitting in my lap as we got back on the highway.

"I'm Glenda," the woman said. "This here's Ken." Ken nodded without looking at me. "We're on our way back from the VA in Albuquerque."

I looked across at Ken, who had the look of a middle-aged soldier about him. "What branch were you in?"

"He was in the Marines. Weren't you, Turkey?"

I looked across to see if Ken was going to take offense. All he did was nod, his eyes still on the road in front of him. This was, apparently, a pet name, not an insult.

"We went up so they could take a look at his back. It looks like he's going to need another operation. And we took a little vacation on the way. We've been camping the last few nights."

She shifted a little, tried to get at least a little more comfortable with my tire in the back of her neck and her head tilted off the low ceiling.

"Well, it's good luck for me that you came along just now."

She shushed me. "Glad to help," she said.

During the sixty miles that she rode straddling the console, twisted sideways, I found out that Ken had had four back operations after serving in the Marines during Vietnam, that Glenda worked for MHMR, a Texas agency that worked with mentally ill and mentally challenged, "For a little while longer, at least," she said. "I haven't been able to go to work all the time lately. Neck problems."

I looked up at her head, twisted, and her face, also twisted.

"Please trade me places," I said, thinking, *my God, look at what I've done.* "That can't be good for you."

"Oh," she said, shushing me again. "It's just for a little while."

So, wedged as we were against each other, there were no secrets. I found out that she expected to lose her job because she couldn't travel like she used to with her neck hurting — if state budget cuts didn't take her job first. That there used to be a VA hospital closer to their home in a small town in West Texas, but it had closed down — federal budget cuts — and now they had to drive all the way to Albuquerque. Although they'd camped out to avoid expensive hotels, it had cost them a hundred dollars to take Ken up to see the VA doctor, and I knew without having to be told that a hundred dollars was a whole lot of money for them.

Sharing begets sharing. I told Glenda that I'd just come off the longest, hardest bout with depression in my life, and she told me that Turkey had had lots of troubles with depression and anxiety since the war. I looked across at Ken. He nodded and kept driving.

Glenda told me about a thing she would do with Ken when things got bad for him. She talked me through a visualization — right there in the car, while she straddled the console — where she encouraged me to imagine a place or a thing that felt safe and secure, and put myself there. For her it was lying underneath a giant oak tree, birds singing in the branches. What I imagined as she talked me through it was a campsite next to the Trampas River, the water burbling, the sun breaking through the tall trees.

What Ken imagined, he did not say.

"Remember that," she said when we were done. "If you're ever feeling like you're not safe, like something bad's going to happen, just go to your safe place until the bad things are gone."

"You're really good at this," I told her, because she clearly had a gift for helping people. I wish someone had helped me in this way when I really needed a safe place, even if it was only in my head. "It would be a crime if you didn't get to keep working with people who need help."

"Whenever God closes a door, he opens a window," she said, and she smiled sadly. "Only so far I can't see any window." Her face was naked for a moment, and I could see her pain and fear for an instant before she shushed herself. "Not that I mean to talk derogatively," she said.

When we reached Roswell, home, as you may know, of purported alien space landings, they took me straight to — yes, God, I am listening — Wal-Mart, the only place still open where

I could get a new tire. It was getting dark, and Ken and Glenda still had a long way to go, so I encouraged them to head on if they needed to, but they waited while I got a new tire mounted on the wheel.

Then Glenda said, "Ken's going to drive you back to change your tire. Isn't that right, Turkey?"

Ken nodded. Out of the car he was huge, and how a bear like him fit behind the wheel of that tiny car was something nigh on miraculous.

"No," I said, and it felt like a real protest. It was 120 miles out of their way. Although it would be a hardship, especially after buying a new tire, I could get a rental or figure something out. "Really, you've been a huge help."

And also, frankly, the idea of driving for an hour alone with Ken, taciturn and disturbed Vietnam vet, was a little troublesome to me too.

"It's decided," she said, and for her, it certainly was.

So I gassed up their tiny car at a truck stop, where she settled in to wait for Ken to return, and Ken and I drove north out of Roswell into the fading light.

I'd have to say I'm among the world's worst with small talk, but I was a little nervous, and I think he was a little nervous, and we hadn't been sitting in silence for very long before I realized that we were having a conversation. Ken had left the Corps in 1988. The CIA had offered him a job, but he'd started driving semi trucks instead.

"I didn't want to do no more of that stuff," he said.

One of my dark secrets is that I interviewed with the CIA twice, back in the days when I was working on my PhD and was still married to Jake's mom, who thought it was about time I got a regular job. I told Ken the story, which is a pretty good one. I'd been thinking about being an intelligence analyst, but finally, after getting through the six-month FBI background check, the physical, and the psychological profile, I couldn't pass the polygraph. Before we started, my examiner asked me to tell him every bad thing I had ever done up to the moment I arrived in their parking lot, and I came up with so many — mostly juvenile misdemeanors, vandalism, and minor property damage, I feel compelled to add — that toward the end he was just sitting there laughing, his hand over his eyes. Although he then constructed the test to omit every one of those things I'd told him — "Since you came into the building today, have you stolen any concrete birdbaths from anyone's yard?" — I failed every single question he asked me.

Including the one about my name.

He kept me there, hour after hour in the basement of CIA headquarters, because he knew I was telling the truth and he thought maybe he could recalibrate the thing, but I went on failing every question they asked me.

"I've never passed a polygraph," I told Ken. "Don't think I even can. I think it's something physiological, maybe something about body electricity, but you can't get a security clearance without a successful polygraph, whatever that means. Or a minimum-wage job in a record store."

Ken laughed, and it gave me some courage to ask. "What kind of work did the CIA want you to do?"

He shook his head, involuntarily, it seemed, and we drove on in silence for a while.

I looked out my window. If it was all the way dark when we got back, it was going to be hard to change that tire, and it was getting darker by the minute.

"I done black ops in Vietnam," he said, all at once, and he was not bragging, just matter of fact, maybe even a little sad. "Operating behind enemy lines. One time we went 200 miles over the border into China to assassinate a general. Another time they sent us to do a job in Hanoi."

He looked straight ahead, drove silently for a while. Clearly there were other things he could have told me, but he chose not to, as much for his own peace of mind as for mine. When he broke the silence, you could see that he was trying to find a positive in his experience. "One time my buddy got hit. I carried him out. Must have been twenty miles."

"You didn't leave people behind," I said, and it wasn't really a question. I could see this was one of the things he had carried with him, one of the things that had helped him to hold onto himself in the years since he came back.

"No," he said. "We never did."

I nodded. Although I was the first male in my family for at least three generations not to serve in the military, I have always admired those who did serve. And I came close, actually, not even counting the CIA. Thanks to the friendly job counseling of Jake's mom, I had once had a slot in Air Force Officer Candidate School, but they couldn't give me flight training, and they couldn't give me military intelligence, and when all they had available for me was missile command, which was just what you think, sitting in a shielded missile silo and waiting for the end of the world, I told them to give my slot to someone else. And although I have since become a pacifist because I don't think Jesus likes for us to kill each other, from the time I was a tiny kid I've read about wars and men in battle and about the incredible sacrifices they make, and I still have nothing but admiration for our men and women in uniform.

And there I was, sitting with someone who came home injured from a war we sent him to fight — he was now on full disability — and tortured, and while if I'd been old enough back then I probably would have been marching in peace rallies while he was sloshing through dark jungles, in that moment I was fixed with a strange desire to salute him.

What I did instead was tell him, "Thank you. For your service. I know that you went through a lot of really hard things. And I want you to know that I'm grateful you went."

He nodded, almost to himself, and when he spoke, that too was almost to himself. "I slept with my KaBar under my pillow the first year I was home," he said. "I couldn't talk about it until I met Glenda."

"She has a real gift," I said.

We drove on a little farther. We were getting close to my car, and I was watching on the other side of the road for it when he turned to me, the light from the dash illuminating the left side of his face.

"I did what I was ordered to," he told me, and then he turned his head back to watch the road. "A lot of those things weren't very nice." He cleared his throat, and his voice was almost apologetic when he said, "It's different when you're in a war."

I nodded to show that I understood and that I forgave, and then, there was my car.

He pulled around behind it, headlights on for illumination, and then when he saw how wobbly my jack was, he braced himself and his bad back against the rear panel of the car like Hercules while I jacked it up and changed the tire.

"Thank you," I said when we were done, and it was a thank you that spilled off in every direction. Thank you for your help. Thank you for the things you endured. Thank you for trusting me with a piece of your life that you don't show around to just anybody.

He shook my hand, nodded once, and folded himself back behind the wheel of his tiny car.

I followed him back to Roswell. When he pulled into the truck stop to pick up Glenda, he raised a hand as I drove past. I drove on through the night, thinking.

I was thankful, and saddened, and more than a little ashamed. Because, although I am dense, I do not require a whole bookful of attempts to get me to eat green eggs and ham.

I could see the lesson from the moment I had gotten into the car with them, a car I would not have gotten into for any other reason but that I desperately needed help.

These were Samaritans who had pulled over to rescue me. I would never have made their acquaintance in a million years if they hadn't stopped to help me, and if I'd seen them on the side of the road in dire straits, I think more likely than not I would have shook my head in momentary sympathy and kept driving.

"Those are not my people," is what I would have been saying to myself. Or "I don't have time." Or "You don't know what kind of people you might meet in places like this. It might be dangerous."

The night before he was murdered, Dr. King told this same story of the Good Samaritan to a group of people assembled in Memphis to take on a difficult and frightening task. And when he finished, he told them he thought he knew why those first two people, good holy people just like me, had walked right past the wounded man lying beside the road. It was because they were scared.

"And so," Martin said, "the first question that the Levite asked was, 'If I stop to help this man, what will happen to me?' But then the Good Samaritan came by. And he reversed the question: 'If I do not stop to help this man, what will happen to him?'"[2]

That's the question that, knowingly or not, Ken and Glenda had asked and answered when they saw me lugging my tire down the road. They had proven themselves to be neighbors to me, and more. "Come stay with us tonight," Glenda had said before Ken and I went off. "Or anytime. You're always welcome. And don't forget that exercise I taught you. It can be a help in hard times."

Well, what can you say to that kind of radical hospitality?

All you can do is say thank you, and accept it, and pass it on.

"Go and do the same," I think is what Jesus said, and that sounds like a plan to me.

soul

The great call to conversion: to look not with the eyes of my
own low self-esteem, but with the eyes of God's love.

HENRI NOUWEN, *RETURN OF THE PRODIGAL SON*

When I was a kid, my family followed my dad around
the South as he climbed the corporate ladder, from
Oklahoma, where I was born, to Texas, to Georgia, to North
Carolina. It was in North Carolina, at Rama Road Elementary
School, that I first remember being myself — not just some
random memories that may or may not be planted, but actual
memories of what it felt like to be me, to walk around in my
skin, what I liked, what I feared. And it was there, in that newly
integrated elementary school, alongside my black friends bused
in from across town, that I discovered my love, my longing, for
soul music, in fact, for all things African American.

At one time or another, looking over my life, I have wanted
to sing like the young Michael Jackson, to dance like the
Temptations, to play hoops like Julius Erving.

It's not surprising really. Both my parents, God bless them,
are from tiny towns in Oklahoma, and my family could not

have been more white if we'd been spray painted. My dad had one Nat King Cole album — very cool — but a dozen albums by Johnny Mathis, who struck me as the only black singer white enough for most white people to love him.

We know that kids often react against their upbringing, which, as I've intimated, was a little Caucasian. But it was more than that. Although I don't remember names or faces, I remember thinking that the black kids were the arbiters of cool. That I wanted to be like them. And I suppose this isn't a bad thing, on the surface — it would be nice if more people admired and wanted to be a member of a populace that others routinely villainize and victimize.

But the thing is, I wasn't doing it as some way of balancing the social scales or out of a sense of solidarity with people of color suffering oppression. I mean, I was only six or seven then. I wanted to be black because I didn't feel comfortable in my own skin. Because I didn't like who I was.

Because I wanted to be someone else.

Black people had soul. I didn't. Simple as that.

This little self-esteem jones was not, as you've seen, the most toxic of my psychoses, but looking back now, I can see how it runs quietly in the background of all the louder problems, a throbbing backbeat to my guilt, my depression, my inability to accept love or praise as my due. Most of my life, until very recently, I've done what I thought I needed to do — and more — to get people to accept me, to value me, to think I was pretty great — and they did.

But until recently, I didn't — couldn't — accept it myself. All I could ever see was that I needed to do something else, something more, something better, and maybe that would make me feel okay in my own skin.

My parents, of course, are appalled when they hear me say things like this about my past. My mom wants to know how I got this way, as if it were her fault, maybe.

My own inclination has always been to think of my various psychic ailments as part of the artists' condition. Of course, I haven't figured all this out: Are artists drawn to pain, do they feel alienated because of who they are and how they see the world? Or do they feel the pain and move from it to create art and express themselves?

Chicken. Egg. It doesn't matter. What matters is that I have always been this way, that when I think of myself in the first and second grades at Rama Road Elementary, I'm already uncomfortable being the brilliant little kid that I was, and I wanted to be somebody different.

If my parents did somehow screw me up, well, they didn't mean to. So it probably wasn't that they left me screaming in my crib when I was eighteen months old or that they showed those cute naked baby pics around at my birthday party. What they taught me, they taught me as a way of making my way in the world: Don't make too much of yourself — other people won't like you if you do.

It was my church that taught me not to make *anything* of myself, that I was a worthless and deeply flawed creature worthy only for hellfire and damnation. I don't know that Brother Raymond knew he was scarring me for life when he said these things from the pulpit; I'd like to think if he'd known what all that stuff was going to do to me, he might have been a little more careful.

All of which is to say that I am now probably screwing

Chandler up in ways he will not recognize for twenty years, and while I may be paying attention to self-esteem issues and communication issues and intimacy issues — all the things that have tripped me up in my waking life — I'm probably missing something neither of us knows about that will send him running to therapy in later years: "Dad, didn't you realize how important algebra is in the modern world? How come we never talked about it?"

But I digress.

Here's what I loved about the artists of soul from the very beginning. They could sing. No, they wailed.

And when they danced, it wasn't the herky-jerky spastic white-boy dance I conjured into being, but something smooth, stylish, a beautiful expression of their inner selves.

And the world they sang? It was extraordinary, exotic, splendid. Was there ever anyone tougher or cooler than Isaac Hayes' "Shaft" or Curtis Mayfield's "Superfly"?

Where else but soul music could a lover's spat turn into the O'Jays' "992 Arguments"?

Or a breakup into the end of the world, as in the Stylistics' "You Are Everything," or into an anthem of eternal faithfulness like the Four Tops' "Reach Out (I'll Be There)," or into an I-guess-I-showed-you end-zone victory dance like the Delfonics' "Didn't I Blow Your Mind (This Time)."

And love. Admittedly, I was young, but I kissed my first girl when I was five, and had my first girlfriend when I was six. Love has always been on my mind. Soul music tracked the progress from love's butterfly-in-the-stomach beginnings — the Spinners' "Could It Be I'm Falling in Love," to pride of ownership in the Temptations' "My Girl," to the

sheer wonder of it all — the Stylistics' "Betcha By Golly Wow."
It was like my emotional palette had suddenly been given a
hundred vivid colors. I saw the world in a new and different
way. Sometimes when the music was playing, I could even see
myself in a different way.

So perhaps it's not just "soul" that I'm speaking of when I
talk about my love for the music; perhaps it's also grace — the
grace that I received from it.

At the end of Woody Allen's film *Manhattan*, and then also
in the film *Hannah and Her Sisters*, Allen's character describes
some things that make life worth living, the suffering worth
continuing to endure, things like the jazz of Louis Armstrong
and the comedy of the Marx Brothers and the smile of a beautiful woman.

Soul. Beauty. Grace.

These were the kinds of moments I had struggled toward
and sometimes achieved when I myself sang, which I began to
do publicly as a ten-year-old, and later in my writing, my teaching, and, I hope, my preaching: moments of honest expression
that also proved to somehow move those who heard me or read
my works.

As I have said, it was only recently that I began to value
those moments and myself as the creator of them, but somehow despite all those years in which Bad Mind, as Anne Lamott
calls it, held sway in my cranium, I managed to do good work.
Like Clay Forester, the narrator of my novel *Free Bird*, I took up
music mostly to get girls, but somewhere along the way magical
things happened.

Longtime members of my church growing up might
remember my singing and playing piano there as a 'tween, teen,

and twentysomething. In Mustang, Oklahoma, where I went to high school, I am still modestly famous for my portrayal of Conrad Birdie in the high school production of *Bye Bye Birdie* over twenty years ago.

People did love to hear me sing.

Of course, none of that registered. For most of my life, as I've mentioned, respect and regard slid off me like water off a duck.

Maybe it's also as Parker Palmer has said, that the things that others seemed to value in me seemed to come so easily to me that I couldn't value them myself. Maybe I figured, you might as well think I'm great because I'm nice-looking or because I'm smart — two more things I didn't have much of anything to do with making possible.

So how did things change? Because like almost all the horrible things I write about in this book, they did change, or I wouldn't be here to write about them.

Well, maybe it came with Roy Orbison, the sad white troubadour from Wink, Texas. Or the white bluesman Stevie Ray Vaughn. What I heard in their voices, in Stevie's guitar, were the same things I had always heard from the Temptations and the O'Jays.

Soul. Grace.

Clearly these were people who had been hurt — and were, perhaps, still hurting. But their music grew out of their painful experience, and the beauty of it beautified it. And, of course, they both died in the middle of their messages, and even at my most heathen, I still recognized that the death of a suffering prophet was a sacred event, one to be mused over and memorialized.

Later there were other kindred musical spirits who sang

my thoughts and feelings and through their gifts, made them beautiful and bearable: Bruce Hornsby, Bruce Springsteen, Bob Schneider, Shawn Colvin.

But not all of the beautiful music in the world taught me how to love myself, to accept myself in all my can't dance, can't rap, can't dunk whiteness.

What it took, really, was a miracle, and while there was music involved, it wasn't only music.

Sometime during the spring of 2001, I read an essay about screenwriter Bill Broyles in *Texas Monthly*, and as an aside, it talked about a historically African-American church where he — a white guy — was a prominent member. It described the black gospel music, the multicultural community, and although at that point the mere idea of being inside a church shook me, I remember looking up the address of St. James Episcopal in the yellow pages and writing down the service times in my journal.

I actually drove by the church after that, although I'm not sure what possessed to me to drive out MLK to check it out.

But some months later, after knowing that I was supposed to visit there, that if I did, something important would happen, I showed up for the 10:15 Sunday service.

The church was smallish, roundish, filled with people of every color and persuasion. I sat in the very back, where I fought off a panic attack brought on by being a stranger in the middle of so many people, by my sitting in the pew of a church again after so many years and so much hard mileage.

The Episcopal service was unfamiliar to me. I didn't know what to do, but I acted as though I knew what book to open when, what prayer to chant. The rector, Greg Rickel, was white, but he seemed cool enough. In his sermon he quoted the Persian mystic poet Rumi and the *Reformed Jewish Book of Prayer*. I was impressed. The Nicene Creed was familiar and I could read along, although at that point I wasn't sure I believed a word of it.

And then, toward the end of the service, I stood up to take communion. I didn't expect to. I didn't know what to expect, really. I didn't know Episcopalians took communion. I thought all they did was drink and play golf.

But as Greg stood in front of us, behind the altar set with bread and wine, he said something that changed my life: "Wherever you are in your journey of faith, you are welcome at this table."

Surely, I thought, he doesn't mean me. He wouldn't have said that if he'd known I was out here. It's only for the cool people, the good people, the people who belong.

But I didn't want people to look at me like I didn't know what I was doing, so I stood when everyone else did, walked down to the front of the church, watched my neighbors closely. I knelt. I held out my hand for the wafer. I sipped the wine from the chalice.

And I went home.

Now I can't say that this was like some magic spell, because I didn't suddenly realize that I was okay. I didn't immediately feel self-actualized, whatever that would feel like.

But all of a sudden, I had some new kids to emulate. I practiced crossing myself in front of the mirror until I felt I wouldn't make an ass of myself. And week after week, whenever I wasn't out of town on book tours or doing workshops, I showed up at St. James.

Some Sundays were better than others. Sometimes I sat in the back and shivered, felt like the only person on the planet, even surrounded by these wonderful people.

But most days, I listened to the voices.

The people at St. James — red and yellow, black and white — had soul.

They sang African-American hymns like Andrae Crouch's "Soon and Very Soon" and Isaiah Jones' "God Has Smiled on Me." At baptisms, they sang spirituals like "Take Me to the Water" and "Wade in the Water." At Christmas, there was "Rise Up, Shepherd and Follow," and sometimes at communion they sang "I'm a-Going to Eat at the Welcome Table."

They sang beautifully. Better, even. They wailed. They clapped along to the old spirituals. Their faces radiated joy. Love.

Welcome.

Open communion, which is what Greg was announcing my first Sunday and every Sunday since, is a huge theological issue I have since come to understand. Some of my close friends in seminary think of it as an abomination, or something close to it.

All I can say is that open communion beckoned me toward belonging when I didn't even feel welcome in my own skin. If sacraments are outer signs of inward grace, then open communion represented God's radical love and acceptance of even messed-up me.

And so did the people of St. James, who week after week greeted me, passed me the peace, loved me back into health. Georgetta and Carolyn, who didn't know me from Adam when I first showed up, hugged me every week, and when they wished me "the peace of Christ," I could almost feel peace.

I love you. God loves you.

I had prayed for help. I had told God — or whatever passes for God — that I was at the end of my rope. That I couldn't stand being me anymore. That I was out of solutions and I was handing over the controls.

And I had sat back and waited for a miracle.

You know, there's an old preacher's joke about these people who have climbed up on the roof of their house because a flood is raging through the town. Devout people, much more religious than I ever was, although not as religious as I may someday be. But these people prayed for divine intervention, and when a guy in a rowboat stopped by and offered to help, even though the water was rising higher, they sent him away. And when the police came in a motorboat, even though the water was lapping at the eaves, they sent him away. And when a rescue helicopter hovered overhead, even though the water was at their thighs, they sent it away. Because they were waiting for a miracle.

And as the joke goes, finally they get swept away and they drown. Funny, huh? And when they get to the Pearly Gates, they're like totally pissed.

"God," they say, "how could you let us die like that? We prayed for you to save us, and we believed in you a hundred percent."

And God just shakes God's head — if God has a head — and says something like, "You idiots! What were you waiting for? I sent you two boats and a helicopter!"

I had been waiting for a big-time miracle, a magic wand waving overhead that would change the way I thought about myself.

But one Sunday morning I looked up and around, and I saw

God looking back at me from the face of everyone I saw at St. James, heard God speaking in Greg's words, felt God's embrace in every passing of the peace.

And I finally understood: I had always been loved. Always been accepted. Always been valued. And always had a soul worth saving.

When it doesn't matter who you are, what you've done, or what you didn't do — that is true hospitality, true grace, true love. When everyone is welcome at the table, then anyone is welcome at the table.

As I write these words I discover that I again have tears in my eyes from the sheer wonder of it all. Of course, it doesn't hurt that the music I'm writing to is this ecstatically sad soul music from the seventies, Blue Magic's "Let the Sideshow Begin."

It's passionate and extravagant and over the top, just like my ridiculously overcomplicated life has been. But you know what? None of that history, of that Bad Mind, matters anymore, because, at last, I know I belong. I'm part of something bigger than myself, and it makes me want to sing.

I am welcome at God's table, and miracle of miracles, my soulful brothers and sisters have saved a place for me.

credo

Faith is not a blind conformity to a prejudice. . . . It is a decision, a judgment that cannot be proven. It is not merely the acceptance of a decision that has been made by somebody else.

THOMAS MERTON, *NEW SEEDS OF CONTEMPLATION*

At around eleven o'clock every Sunday morning at St. James, we rise after the conclusion of the sermon and speak in one voice. Some of us read from the *Book of Common Prayer*. Others speak from memory, eyes closed. But at every Eucharist, we repeat a creed, which comes from the Latin "credo," which means "I believe."

If I'm a eucharistic minister, one of the lay leaders of the service, it's my job to lead. I rise when I see Greg stand up, and then, clad in a floor-length black robe called a cassock and a white outer robe called a surplice, I say, in my good loud speaking-to-the-public voice, "Let us affirm our faith in the words of the Nicene Creed."

And then I begin: "We believe in one God, the Father, the Almighty, Maker of Heaven and Earth."

The Nicene Creed is one of the two universal creeds used

in many Christian denominations. It was produced at a church council in Asia Minor—what is now Turkey—in the year 325, at the behest of the Roman Emperor Constantine, who had converted to Christianity but remained more than a little disturbed about the fact that thinkers and leaders of this religion he'd walked into kept arguing with each other about pieces of doctrine. This particular piece of doctrine they were arguing about was actually pretty important: Was Jesus a human being who became God, or was he God from before the beginning of the world? It had implications over how people conceived of God, and it had implications about how Jesus brought salvation.

The bishops who convened at Nicaea were of all sorts of opinions, from the two extremes and scattered across the middle. At the end, with the emperor looking over their shoulders, all but three of the bishops signed the creed, and the belief that Jesus was God and always had been became official doctrine within the church. Religious historian Karen Armstrong writes, "The show of agreement pleased Constantine, who had no understanding of the theological issues, but in fact there was no unanimity at Nicaea. After the council, the bishops went on teaching as they had before."[1]

Why would all these leaders holding different opinions have come together to create a document they could say—but didn't all entirely believe? Well, in this case, of course, it seemed important to be able to show their agreement to someone outside the church, in this case, Constantine. But there's something else, some kind of unanimity that came in the face of their diversity when they all agreed to say they believed the same things at least for the time that they were standing together.

My first regular exposure to the Nicene Creed as a part of worship came in 1997, when Tinamarie and I attended a progressive Presbyterian church in Eugene, Oregon, where we lived while I was teaching at the University of Oregon and working on a book that may never be finished. Lots of denominations besides Episcopalians and Presbyterians are creedal. And even growing up in the Southern Baptist Church, one of my favorite songs at Falls Creek youth camp in Oklahoma was called "I Believe," and began, "I believe in God the Father. I believe in Christ the Savior."

You better believe we didn't sing about the "one holy catholic and apostolic church," which is toward the end of the Nicene Creed, but still, this too was a creedal statement.

When I first began hearing the Nicene Creed in Oregon in 1997, I discovered that I couldn't speak it out loud. There were parts I was down with, true, but other parts I just absolutely could not get my lips around. I'm not the only one who at times has found the creed a stumbling block. The unorthodox but popular retired Episcopal bishop John Shelby Spong devoted the entire first chapter of his book *Christianity Must Change or Die* to deconstructing the Nicene Creed: I don't believe this. I don't think anyone was ever meant to take this literally. And you'd have to be *crazy* to believe this.

There are, even as rabidly Christian as I have to admit to being now, still parts of the creed that I'm not sure I believe literally. And yet every Sunday — and during the week at the seminary chapel — I say the Nicene Creed or its fraternal twin the Apostle's Creed. And you know what?

Doubt or not, I believe it.

When I asked Greg for some guidance about the creeds,

his words, as always, were comforting to me. In his long e-mail back he wrote,

> The statement I like to make, and truly believe, about the creeds, Apostle's and Nicene, is that they are truer today than when they were written. I say this because they come today with all the words, intentions, tears, prayers, human interaction, and recitation that have been added to them through time.
>
> To me the creeds are the melody of Christianity. They're like tunes we know the minute we hear them. For some the words are exact and factually true, but I don't think they have to be. For many, they are true in the Native American way of truth, but for all of us they are a set of words that tell a story designed to point to Truth with a capital "T." The words may not be factually true, but the basic story or narrative is true, and what they point to is a Truth of God.
>
> So, I don't struggle with saying the creeds. Our scientific enlightenment often gets in the way of the mystery that is, and always will be, our way to God.

My friend Dave, who went through confirmation class with me, has a friend who says he'll believe anything if he can sing it. For me, it's a matter of story, and if it's a story that moves me to belief, I can accept it, even with holes in the plot you could drive a truck through. Like in *Die Hard 2*, how come nobody thought to reroute all those planes to another airport instead of having them circle DC until they fell out of the sky?

But if you give yourself to a story, if you let yourself feel it and let it touch you, if you're truly in it, you have to believe it. When Jake was about ten years old, I remember driving him and his friends, Van and Daniel, out to Daniel's house, the three of them wedged in the backseat of my little putt-putting Volkswagen Jetta singing "Bingo," and when I looked back at them and saw how they were singing and clapping and shaking the car, I think, at least in that moment, we had a car full of people who believed there was a farmer who had a dog and Bingo was his name-o.

Finally, we come back again to faith: I believe. As I always say, stories are how we make sense of our experience. And the truth is, our lives are made up of stories we've chosen to be our own stories. About ourselves: I'm good at math but lousy at languages. About our families: We're the most different people you could imagine, but in a pinch, we pull together. About our world: America is a fortress of freedom and democracy, and the French people smell funny because they eat them funny cheeses.

The stories we own tell us who we are and what we're supposed to be doing. Sometimes we hold on to those stories even against logic or evidence because we need them. One time Rodger Kamenetz and I were on a panel at a literary festival, and he talked about how in the Jewish rabbinical tradition the great rabbis were always great storytellers. Their gift, he said, was that they could look at you and see what story you needed to hear to be healed. And as usual, I think he's onto something.

When I was having trouble saying the creed, it wasn't because I didn't believe in God, although, like I've said, during my twenties and thirties I believed in God like I believed in aluminum, like something you read about. What was happening was that the creed had not become my story yet, and because it wasn't my story yet, I was still really bothered by those aluminum airliners still up there improbably circling the airport.

Kathleen Norris tells a story in *Amazing Grace* about a bright seminary student and an Orthodox priest discussing the creed. The student kept asking, "How can I repeat the Creed when I don't believe it all?" and the priest kept saying, "If you keep saying it, eventually, you'll own it."[2]

And Lauren Winner, in her own chapter called "Credo" — and before you report me to the literary police, I think Lauren may have cribbed it from somewhere else too, so I'm not feeling guilty — wrote about her own conflict by saying that the creed is more about relationship than knowledge. "It is about a promise to believe even when you don't," she says, and she likens it to our vow to love our spouse in marriage, a vow that isn't necessarily about feeling "smitten every morning," but is about continuing in relationship in good times and bad.[3]

I've tried to tell you how I entered into that relationship, how gradually I came to the point of wanting more God than I could find in a book, how I needed another story to be healed because none of the stories I had were working for me anymore. You've seen how my writing taught me that what I believed in, deep down, was the power of redemption and faith and hope.

What happened to me at last, was that I decided I needed to believe in this story like my life depended on it, because, by that time, it did.

And while "story" sounds dismissive — like the way we think the word "myth" means something untrue instead of something absolutely true that we just can't prove with a set of calipers and a slide rule — we ultimately choose the stories we base our lives on not because of their historical evidence but because of how they make us feel and what they help us understand.

It's important to notice that we're not talking necessarily about a one-size-fits-all story, although that's what the Emperor Constantine was hoping for. Not everybody needs the same story to be healed. The Christian story that I received when I was a child was toxic to me, a story I couldn't inhabit without tremendous damage to myself. And yet, clearly, it's a story that brings comfort to many people, and in its outlines, at least, it was a story that I wanted to believe.

Since I thought that was the only Christian story, I went looking for other stories. I rummaged through the bookshelves of the world, so to speak. Along the way I found many things that were appealing to me. I was tremendously attracted to the teachings of Buddhism, which often reinforced what I had appreciated about some versions of the Christian story I'd heard — compassion, justice, and mindfulness. I read Jewish history and theology very seriously, as though I might be converting next Thursday. But I never found the story with my name on it, because, at heart, there was only one story meant for me, and I'd already gotten a glimpse of it. Although the Dalai Lama is one of the world's leading teachers of Buddhism, he typically tries to dissuade people from leaving their home traditions to follow another, including his, even if they find valuable teachings in other faith stories. I think there is wisdom in this. He suggests that we can learn from other faiths, as he did about Christianity from Thomas Merton, and yet "remain firmly committed to our own faith. This way is best."[4]

It certainly has been for me. I learned things about compassion, mysticism, and awareness from Buddhism, and about justice and holiness from Judaism, and when the Christian story I needed to hear finally caught me, I was able to bring these things along.

It was MLK and Thomas Merton and Dorothy Day and Will Campbell — Christian social activists who loved and served God through others — and Dennis Covington and Anne Lamott and Bret Lott and Lee Smith — Christian literary writers who loved and served God through their art — who told me the Christian story again in a way I could embrace. And it was St. James and the Episcopal Church that gave me communion and a family story I could accept.

So my story was, after all, a Christian story, and I began to declare myself to be Christian, although that also was freighted with baggage from before. Not everybody likes Christians, and I don't just mean in terms of some sort of religious persecution. My girlfriend, R., for example, could not at first understand what on earth might possess someone to even go to a seminary.

"Doesn't it get tiresome," she asked, "being around Christians all day?"

And you could be offended by that remark, although she meant no harm by it. Or you could recognize that her understanding of what Christians are sometimes like is a pretty common one outside the walls of the ark. It's the same sentiment I used to have toward people who went to the trouble of identifying themselves as Christian. I thought that at best they'd be tiresome. And at worst, they'd be judgmental, small-minded, petty, or mean.

Because I write about religion a lot, and I teach at a Christian university, and I'm attending seminary, media people often treat me as though I'm a representative Christian. "What do Christians think about this?" is a question I sometimes get.

(And my answer, by the way, is usually something like, "Well, I can't speak for all of them, but this Christian thinks — ")

It's not always easy being treated as a representative Christian, because sometimes I get caught in the crossfire of conflicts I don't even know about. One day when I was doing a radio interview for the book Chris and I wrote on *The Matrix* — I should have known this wouldn't go well, since it was a call-in with a Las Vegas shock jock and I could hear that the guest right before I came on was a stripper who had certain exotic talents — the first question I got from the guy once we went on the air was a sneering, "So, you're a Christian."

I knew exactly what he was thinking. In his voice I could hear that I represented every bad thing he had ever felt and thought and experienced about Christians, and for a split second I did think of saying, "Well, yes, I am, but not, apparently, the kind of Christian you think I am."

But you know, it seemed a little too much like Peter denying Jesus the night before the Crucifixion, and I let that idea pass as quickly as it had come.

"Yes," I said. "I am."

That guy hung up on me so hard it left an imprint on my ear drums.

I think my neighbors heard it.

I felt about two inches tall, and part of me wanted to call him back and tell him how badly he had hurt my feelers.

But I also felt like I had told a plain and simple truth and I should feel pretty good about it. Whether you like it or not, I am a Christian. My life is centered around serving God, whatever that means. I believe in God the Father Almighty, Maker of Heaven and Earth.

And so on. And so forth.

This spring, when we had a quiet day at the seminary, a day without regular classes that is totally set aside for reflection, our retreat leader was an Episcopal nun who gave us a set of questions to wrestle with. In answering her question "What are the ideas that have brought you liberation?" in my journal, I discovered that I created my own personal credo, and I hope I can be forgiven if my beliefs combine Jesus, Thoreau, and Spider-Man, as they often do:

> God loves me.
> No one has a monopoly on God.
> God is revealed through Scripture, reason, tradition, nature, and art.
> My hurts can help bring healing to others.
> We serve a God of second chances.
> Act as if you had faith, and faith will be given unto you.
> True greatness, true happiness come from serving others.
> We understand the world through stories.
> With great power comes great responsibility.
> It's okay to march to the beat of a different drummer.
> Want less. Give more.
> You have to love yourself before you can love anybody else.
> Before you can love God.

There are a lot of other things I could say about what I believe, but you know what? Most of them are just my opinions, and I'd probably be saying them to be contentious, and since I don't want to be a contentious person, I'll settle for this last story of what I believe Christianity is about.

When I show the movie *Magnolia*, which has been a great and transformative experience for many of my students at Baylor, there's always at least one student — and it's always a devout young lady, and I don't mean to be stereotypical, but it is — who comes up to me either after we've watched the film or who writes in her journal and says, "I was tremendously offended by the _____ in this movie, and I can't believe that you made me watch it. I'm a good Christian, and I would never in my life have anything to do with people like that."

(Which is to say people who are alone or broken or hurting, like the characters of this great film, and who are anesthetizing themselves with drugs or alcohol or rage or sex.)

And, as gently as I can, I always respond, "You know, I guess Jesus didn't get that memo. Because he ate with sinners and tax collectors, and he said he'd come not to minister to the well, but to the sick. To the broken. To the hurting."

I always tell them that Jesus loves everybody, that he in fact loves people like those people just as much as he loves good Christians.

So this is my last big item of belief: God is love, and Jesus came to show us that. His message wasn't a bunch of thou-shalt-nots, like you often hear in sermons. It was love: Love each other, love your God.

Maybe, bookended the way the Gospels are by the Mosaic Law and by Paul's rule-making, people forget that Jesus told more stories than he gave rules, and the big one Jesus left was this: "This is my commandment, That ye love one another, as I have loved you."[5]

On this side of the veil, we're told our understanding is imperfect, and for that reason, I think it's important to remember that love is the most important thing, more important than doctrine, more important than what we think people should or should not be doing. And if we put that into effect, here are some examples of what it means:

If you think that gay people don't go to heaven — you understand, by the way, that you're not the one in charge of that — that's fine.

You still have to love them.

If you think the church down the block — or across the ocean — has got it all wrong, it doesn't mean the Devil has led them astray. And you know what?

You still have to love them.

If you think that somebody is a bigot, or a hypocrite, or a closed-minded fundamentalist, that's your opinion.

But you still have to love them.

That's what I love about the Anglican Communion, the loose worldwide affiliation to which the Episcopal Church belongs. Although we're wrestling with very contentious issues just now, historically, the Communion has been a place where different people could hold different opinions about God, about worship, about politics, about whatever, and still come together to say the same Creed. It's been a place of conciliation as well as a place of strong belief.

And it's what I love about the seminary. Among my close friends, there are people who are as liberal as, or more liberal than, I am on theological, political, and cultural issues. And there are others who disagree with me on almost all of those things.

In my Spanish for Ministry class last spring, the professor, Dr. Peña, would ask us about doctrinal or liturgical or political issues, and commonly he would start at the far end of the table, where my friends Ken and Don would be on one side of an issue, then on around the table to where Kevin and I would be on the other, and as we listened to each other trying to form our answers in Spanish, it made us laugh that we think so differently but we all love each other and are close friends and are all in training to serve in the same church and are all so awful at Spanish.

We could let those differences drive us apart — that's what commonly seems to happen in this country, with religion, culture, and politics. We could even demonize each other, as some folks do to those who disagree with them or believe differently.

Or we could see each other as Christians who all love God and are trying to serve God, and we could forgive each other over and over, even to seventy times seven, the way Jesus said we should.

And we could have parties, which is what you should do, especially with those you disagree with.

I hated the people of my old church in Oklahoma for twenty years for the way they made me feel and the things they tried to teach me that pushed me away from God. Hated them. Really. I'm not proud of it, but there it is. It wasn't until just before the events in this book that I began to forgive them.

One night when I had brought Jake home to his mom, before I turned around and headed back to Texas, I stopped at the 7-Eleven down the street from my old church, bought a six-pack of beer, and carried it up onto the old church fire escape I'd known as a kid.

When I was twelve, we used to climb up this fire escape by the metal poles holding it up, like we were Army Rangers; when

I was sixteen, I sat out here with girls and watched the sun set over the pond of the farmland next door.

And lots of times over the years, I came out here and sat just to get away from the people inside.

So that night I sat out there on the fire escape, and I drank beer, and I started off still feeling resentful and angry and hurt, which is what just coming near these buildings made me feel.

But the curse of being a writer is empathy — sometimes you end up understanding even people who are diametrically opposed to you, even people you don't want to understand, like the time I realized that the reason the highway patrolman in far West Texas was still talking to me long after he'd given me a ticket, despite my annoyance and desire to get back on the road and speed some more, was because he was lonely. The people he pulled over out there in the great expanse of nothing were the only people he got to talk to all day long.

He was the lone ranger.

Empathy — putting yourself inside the shoes of others — softens us. It's hard to go on thinking the worst of people when we see them as people just like us — with different beliefs, maybe, or ways of expressing them, but with the same kinds of loves and human desires we all have. When I see how much my friend De loves his family or Don his, how can I do anything but love them, whether or not we agree exactly on how we ought to conduct a church service?

As I sat on the fire escape drinking beer, the empathy bug hit me again, and it was a breakthrough I'd needed my whole adult life. It suddenly hit me that the people of my church believed what they believed not because they were interested in driving me insane, but because they were trying to get closer to

God. That was why they had gathered in those pews week after week, sung all seven verses of "Just As I Am," done interminable altar calls while Brother Raymond told us to listen to the Holy Spirit — "every head bowed, every eye closed" — to determine if we might be the one person in the congregation who needed to walk down the aisle and come to God.

And the fact that they pushed me so hard to believe as they did but that their beliefs didn't work for me wasn't their fault. We all come to God in different ways, and they were just doing the best they could, in the only way they knew how. It was all they had to offer, and they didn't mean to hurt me.

They didn't mean to hurt me.

In that moment, I forgave them all: the deacons who had scared me, and Glenette, the pastor's daughter, who once at Falls Creek had led a prayer for my salvation with me standing right there in the room, and all the people who had made my mother feel unwelcome because she had divorced my dad and divorce was a sin.

They didn't mean to hurt me was the important phrase I was left with at the end of the evening, and it moved me. I actually bowed my head, closed my eyes, and breathed a prayer of forgiveness — me for them, their forgiveness for me, God's forgiveness for all of us for all the ways we hurt each other, sometimes without knowing it, over what we believe about God.

It had been a wonderful evening, and I felt light, hopeful, in a way I wouldn't again until I got well. Just to have that monkey of anger and misunderstanding off my back for a moment was liberating.

Forgiveness is what Jesus called us to, and it's what we have to do, because forgiveness is the only way we can live together.

You know that from your own life, your own relationship with family or a significant other: Forgiveness is the key.

We don't have to agree with each other on every detail of how we connect to God, any more than the bishops at Nicaea agreed on every detail. But we can agree to love each other, and to forgive each other, and to try to have some things in common that identify us to each other as one in the Lord.

Like the creed.

Like the love of God.

At least, that's what I believe.

obedience

When God calls someone, God makes it work.
It doesn't have to be — and it often isn't — rational.

JOE BARRY, DURING SPIRITUAL DIRECTION

Not long ago, I went to see the Russell Crowe movie *Cinderella Man* with my girlfriend, R. In it, James J. Braddock, the down-on-his-luck prizefighter played by Russell Crowe, promises his eldest son in the darkest days of the Great Depression that he won't let their family be broken up — that he'll do whatever he has to do to protect them. And yet when he's unable to get work and their power gets turned off in the dead of winter, he comes home to discover that his wife has sent the kids off to her sister's house so they don't freeze, and that his promise has been for nothing.

I understand this story and the need to feel like we can protect those we love through the works of our own hands, through our own tenacity. When Chris came back from camp with my goddaughter, Hanna, a few weeks ago, he was distraught that she's gotten too big to go into the bathroom with him when they stop for a potty break. "How can I take care of my daughter if I'm not there to watch over her?" he asked, and I understand his story too, since it's the same one, all over again.

We need to feel that we're in control of our lives and of those lives that matter most to us. It's an illusion — Chris knows that, I know that, and so do you — but still, it's an illusion we find appealing.

Control. It's not just for breakfast anymore.

I've been a father for twenty years now. Of all the things I've been in my life — writer, teacher, speaker, seminarian, bass player for a tone deaf and tremendously obese Elvis impersonator — being a father is the thing of which I'm proudest. Chris would say the same. And Jimmy Braddock wouldn't have done the things he did and let the fool get beat out of him over and over if the same weren't true for him.

So I'm guessing that James J. Braddock and Chris and I — and most of you reading this — would fail the obedience test that the book of Genesis sets for Abraham, that of willingly offering up his child, Isaac, as a sacrifice. If I heard a voice telling me to do something like that with one of my boys, I'd consider it a sign, all right, but mostly a sign that I needed to go back on medication.

I don't think I could be obedient to that kind of call, first, because the God I choose to love and serve has made it clear in the intervening millennia that God doesn't want human sacrifice, that we're supposed to revere human life, that in the person of Jesus, God sent salvation and an example of justice and love that could draw us closer to God than any sacrificial smoke wafting to heaven.

But Abraham didn't get that memo because it hadn't been written yet — and since a part of what we know about God comes from the way Abraham responds to this test, I guess it's all good, although frankly there have been times when I didn't want to serve any kind of God who could even make a request like this.

Bruce Feiler, in his book *Walking the Bible*, calls the Binding of Isaac — the *Akedah*, as it's known in Hebrew — "the first truly interactive moment in the Bible, the first time the reader is forced to ask: 'What would I do in this situation?'"[1] It's not the first moment in Genesis where Abraham is asked to do something — the whole story of Abraham, from the first day that God asks him to set out into the desert and leave his family and the world he knows behind, is about a series of calls and Abraham's response to them. But this is the first time that God has not only said something that doesn't seem to make any sense, but called for a kind of obedience that doesn't make sense.

I find it easier to just push this story aside and say it doesn't have anything to teach me. But you know what? God doesn't always ask things that make good rational sense.

My life is ongoing proof of this.

You see, ultimately this story is less about whether Abraham is willing to offer up his child on the altar and more about whether Abraham is willing to make God the supreme figure in his life and trust that all things will be well in God's appointed time.

Whether Abraham is willing to give up control — or the illusion of control.

And that, I'm sorry to say, is a lesson that is still directly pertinent today.

The Abraham story up to the point I'm describing is pretty well known, but I'll give it to you in case you missed a few installments somewhere along the way: After a series of misadventures and domestic entanglements worthy of "Desperate Housewives," the aged Abraham finally receives his miraculous son and heir, Isaac, and now God's promise to make Abraham's descendants as numerous as the stars of the sky can come true. Hooray!

But sometime after that — the story doesn't specify Isaac's age, but tradition suggests that Isaac was a vigorous young man capable of carrying a heavy load — Abraham receives the message that God wants him to offer his son — his beloved son, the text says, the one you love — as a sacrifice. The next thing the story tells us is that he takes Isaac on a three-day journey away from home, and then atop a mountain that tradition recognizes as the Temple Mount in Jerusalem, Abraham binds Isaac and raises his knife.

That's when the Angel of the Lord jumps in and tells Abraham, "Okay, good work, you pass," and points out a ram tangled in the bushes they can sacrifice to God instead. Then for the seventh and final time in the story, God promises to multiply Abraham's heirs and, more importantly, now to make them a blessing to the entire world "because you have obeyed my voice."

Jewish, Christian, and Muslim scholars have argued about what the story means, and even about the exact elements of it, and that's not surprising. The story is told so starkly, without taking us into the mind of God or of Abraham, that all we have are the surface details, and they may require argument. And what do we take away from it?

Well, that's also been a subject of debate.

A traditional Christian interpretation of the story is that in the persons of Abraham and Isaac we find a type or prefiguring of the sacrifice of Jesus, of the Father in the Christian Testament willing to offer his only and innocent son. Since Paul, Christians have been interpreting events in what they commonly call the Old Testament in light of the events in the story of Jesus. This is the sermon I always heard preached from this text when I was growing up.

But the Binding of Isaac still offers a compelling lesson. It's an example of the willingness to do whatever God asks, of what the Letter to the Romans calls "obedience, which leads to righteousness," no matter how challenging the task might be.[2]

We can also find support for this kind of reading outside of the Christian Testament. Jews celebrate Abraham's faithfulness, of course, but there's nothing else about the binding in the rest of the Hebrew Scriptures. It's not until the rabbis began arguing about the text that another compelling reading appears, and interestingly, while it does have to do with obedience, it doesn't have to do with Abraham.

Jews in the Middle Ages, persecuted on all sides, seized on the character of Isaac as a symbol of God's goodwill even in the face of violence and oppression. For them, as for Christians and Muslims, Isaac was a patriarch, a prophet, but the truth is, when you look at his story in Genesis, Isaac doesn't do much. He's born, he's offered as a sacrifice, a servant goes to another land and brings back a bride for him, he comes together with his half-brother Ishmael to bury Abraham, he's fooled by his son Jacob into giving him a blessing —

It just doesn't look like hall-of-fame patriarch material, does it?

But in Jewish *midrash*, that is, rabbinic commentaries that try to read between the lines of the stories we've been given, many commentators argued that Isaac must have displayed his own courage and faith — his own obedience — by willingly submitting to the test God laid out for his father. I mean, really — if Isaac is actually a young man in his twenties, why is he going to let his hundred-year-old father tie him up and put a knife to his throat? Well, he's not — unless he chooses to.

So in eleventh century Europe when Jews suffered oppression, as always, and were ordered to convert to Christianity or die, many of them actually chose to die, sometimes at their own hands or at the hands of those close to them. A chronicler in the German city of Mainz has reported that as they died, the image of Isaac was in front of them, and that each of them was acting out that righteous sacrifice to which Isaac had first agreed. Like Abraham and like Isaac, these medieval Jewish martyrs believed that the suffering that came their way because of their obedience was a sign of God's favor. As Feiler explains in his book *Abraham*, the rabbis argued that righteous people are often asked to suffer. "Hardship," they said, "is an indication of worthiness, not sin, and only strengthens those who are faithful."[3] So obedience was again the central value — when God calls, you answer "Here I am," as Abraham — and maybe Isaac — did.

Muslims, finally, consider Abraham to be the first human being to submit his entire life to God — and thus the first Muslim, because "Islam" means "submission." In fact, in *Abraham*, Feiler summarizes the Muslim interpretation of the binding in this way: "God wants all humans to sacrifice our profane desires — even parental love — to serve a higher calling," and he quotes an Imam who explains the binding by making it a challenge: "When God asks you to do something, how far are you willing to go? Would you sacrifice as much as they did?"[4]

Now, I don't know about you, but this is the kind of challenge that makes me uncomfortable. I feel like I've already sacrificed plenty, thanks very much. When I've been faced with calls that didn't fit with what I wanted, I've been happy to get all rational and say that Abraham's example doesn't fit my circumstances today, that God clearly doesn't want me to make *that* kind of radical sacrifice.

But then I come clanging up against another radical and ridiculous biblical passage on obedience, the one from the gospel of Matthew in the Christian Testament, which concludes,

> Whoever loves son or daughter more than me is not worthy of me; and whoever does not take up the cross and follow me is not worthy of me. Those who find their life will lose it, and those who lose their life for my sake will find it.[5]

This is a command about living, not about dying, so I can't try to say the thing about the cross means I don't have to deal with this one, either. In the Greco-Roman world, the image of taking up your cross was commonly used by philosophers and teachers as a metaphor for living a challenging but honorable life.[6] So try as I might to duck it, the passages make it clear that obedience is my challenge too — to live in a new way, marked by faith and sacrifice and submission to the callings of God.

Sigh. Submission? Now that's a challenge I've wrestled — and still sometimes wrestle — with.

You've seen the bumper sticker "God is my co-pilot"? Or the variant reading, "Dog is my co-pilot." Both of those are fine as bumper-sticker theology, but they don't go far enough if we're to believe the biblical witness, which calls us to relinquish the controls entirely. I've been trying very hard to do that. But a little over a year ago, after a long stretch where God had me on cruise control, I found myself being asked to do something I did not want to do, something that in fact I found very scary, and I had a little control relapse.

It was a year ago, in the spring of 2004, that I decided at last to act on the strong calling I felt that I was supposed to enter the Episcopal seminary in Austin and the process that might lead to ordination in the Episcopal Church. I'd resisted it for several reasons, but one was logical and logistical: If I pursued that calling, then it seemed more and more clear that God was also calling me to lay a significant part of my life on the altar, namely my career as a tenured professor at Baylor University.

That was a problem. I was and am a divorced father with a son in college and another who depends on my paying child support in a timely fashion, and if I gave up my job at Baylor to pursue the call to seminary, then I didn't see any way I could make it financially.

So I argued with God, which I think is within the scope of the binding story. I imagine that Abraham, who once argued with God about the fate of a city full of people he didn't even know, might have had a few choice words concerning the fate of his beloved Isaac. I had words too, words like, "God, the seminary hasn't even admitted me yet. What if they don't? You know, not everybody likes me as much as you do." And so forth.

And yet all the signs kept saying, "Seminary or Bust."

I sat with the problem for a while. I talked with Greg and Chris, with Tom Hanks and with other people I trusted who have known me well. I walked with it, the way Abraham walks alongside his potential loss for three days on his trek to the spot where the offering takes place.

And then I walked into the office of the provost of Baylor University and told the chief academic officer of the largest Baptist educational institution in the world that I felt a strong call to attend the Episcopal seminary and pursue ordination in the Episcopal tradition, and that although I knew Baylor might not want me to focus on that call for the next three or four years, it was something I felt I had to do — no matter what.

The provost thought about it as he looked across his huge desk at me. He didn't seem shocked or even surprised. At last he told me, "I can see you doing this, Greg. If it's what you feel called to do, then I'll support it."

That would have been enough, to know that as hard as it might be, at least there would be a paycheck and health insurance. But there was more: I had already been granted a sabbatical, which I used this past spring to work on this book and to load up on classes at the seminary. My department chair, who has never, frankly, liked me as much as God does, actually reduced my teaching load, so that when I return to teaching this fall I'll be receiving the same salary for teaching fewer classes. And when a few weeks ago Baylor concluded years of painful and divisive infighting and brought in a new president and higher administration, the new provost agreed to honor his predecessor's ridiculous arrangement with me without a moment's hesitation. "You certainly do keep busy," his e-mail said, and that was that.

It's been like finding the ram in the bush in the binding story. I've been blessed this past year both by the experience of being in the seminary, and by all the little miracles that somehow have allowed it to happen. I couldn't have anticipated — or, rather, what I anticipated was so wrong.

So, surrounded by blessing, it wasn't until recently that I really understood the depth of the sacrifice that God was asking me to make.

It wasn't until this summer that it hit home: Because I am a seminarian, I would have to leave St. James.

St. James has been my home, and the people of the parish have been family to me in some of the most difficult and the most joyful days of my life. But in the spring, the seminary assigned me to do my two years of fieldwork at Calvary Episcopal, a beautiful old church in Bastrop, Texas, starting this fall — and as I reached my last days in the parish, I found myself, again, arguing with God about what I'm willing to lay on the altar.

And as I saw how unwilling I was to leave St. James, the teacher in me observed that here we could see yet another lesson of the binding: what we clutch too tightly pushes God away.

My teacher at the seminary, writer and spiritual director Corinne Ware, has written about the importance of detachment — that is, the importance of recognizing and being willing to relinquish anything that might stand in the way of our connection to God. For her, the story of the rich young ruler whom Jesus told to sell everything he owned is not about whether or not wealth is a good thing, but about detachment. If he hadn't been so attached to his possessions, she says, Jesus wouldn't have needed to ask him to relinquish them.[7] His wealth was the most important thing in his life, a security blanket he carried around instead of an attachment to God.

In the world of New Testament Greek, we're talking about things that are *scandalon* (σξανδαλον), that is, rocks on the path that can cause us to stumble or fall on our way to God. In modern-day America, we might say that we're talking about road construction that forces us to drive out of our lane or out of our way. But however we talk about these things we're attached to, we have to ask ourselves, as Corinne asks about the rich young ruler story, "How would Jesus tailor his teaching to me? What idol would he ask me to jettison?"

Our security blanket can be money or power, professional standing or love. And, I'm forced to admit, it could even be the powerful attachment I have had to an inclusive multicultural Episcopal congregation that meets on East MLK in Austin, Texas. When we are confirmed as Episcopalians, we say that we're choosing to live as a denominational person in what people call a post-denominational world, to act as though God uses the Church with a large C to work in the world. If St. James means so much to me that I'm unwilling to leave it to go where I'm being sent, then I make it more important than the large C Church, and I make my desires more important than my relationship to God.

And that I do not want to do.

And so, a few weeks ago, I preached this sermon about Abraham and obedience and I said good-bye to the people of St. James, at least for a while.

I didn't want to say good-bye, believe me. When I preached at the 10:15 service, my service, Greg advised me to stare over people's heads if I felt myself starting to choke up. I made it through without weeping — but not without feeling great sadness.

And great gratitude.

Four years ago I wrote down the address and service times of St. James Episcopal Church in my journal for reasons I couldn't understand. I didn't really want to walk through the doors of a church, any church, anytime, anywhere. But I knew, somehow, that I was supposed to, that I was called to this place.

Those are the lessons that the story of the binding teaches us: obedience, faithfulness, and surrender. Hard lessons. But what comes of these is joy.

I'm living proof.

I didn't want to leave St. James. But I know that there will be many things for me to learn at Calvary, ways I can serve in that church, people who will be a blessing to me in ways I can't even know. I know that like that miraculous ram in the bush, God has gifts stashed for me there I can't anticipate. By the time you read these words, I'll already be experiencing some of them.

This is what I told the people of St. James just before I left them:

> Although it will be hard, I'm going to try to be faithful: I'm going to go out into the world to pass on the love and acceptance and passion for justice that you have taught me.
>
> Representing you is an honor I will not take lightly.
>
> No matter where I go or what I do, I will never forget that you have been the radiant face of God for me.
>
> May you continue to be a blessing to a world that desperately needs healing and wholeness, and may your hearts be ever filled with the joy of God: Creator, Redeemer, Sustainer.
>
> AMEN.

I had written love letters to women before; I'd written them to my boys. I had never written a love letter to a church.

But then again, in recent years, I've been pleasantly surprised by a lot of things that happened when I simply said, "Here I am."

ORDINATION

orientation

My Lord God, I have no idea where I am going.
I do not see the road ahead of me.
I cannot know for certain where it will end.

THOMAS MERTON

When I arrived at the seminary in July of 2004, I moved into my little garage apartment without the assistance of a single soul except for a helping hand from my neighbor, Rich, moving my bulky new Mexican bookcase up the stairs. It wasn't easy lugging my sofa upstairs, turtle-like, on my back, but Hunt and Roger, my good friends from St. James who would be seminary seniors that fall, were off all day doing CPE, or clinical pastoral education, which is a long way around to say that for twelve weeks they were working as hospital chaplains. I would see them in the evening, Hunt setting the pain of the day aside like a scientist might take off a lab jacket, Roger still living the hard truths he'd seen that day on the ward. He looked tired, haunted, even.

"I baptized a dead baby this week," he told me one Sunday morning in early August as I was getting ready to leave for St.

James and he was letting his dog out. "It was liquid," he told me as Tyke rooted around in the bushes behind us. "If it hadn't been in the blanket, it wouldn't have held together. And I couldn't react to that. I had to set the tone."

"Wow," I said, impressed and appalled all at once. Liquid.

"I can't wait until the day I get to baptize live babies," he sighed.

Those were the kind of war stories they brought home every day. There was the afternoon when one of Hunt's patients — a woman suffering from "every disease known to man" — died, lay in the room for hours, and then started to dissolve — Dissolve! — as they waited to release the body to her son. Finally he arrived, and he went inside the room while Hunt and the funeral director waited outside. He was in there for half an hour, and there was screaming and yelling, presumably coming from him.

"They had issues," his sister explained.

Or Hunt's patient from his first week of CPE, an African-American woman who had been set on fire by her husband, and had endured operations and illness and fourteen months in the hospital, but had never lost her faith or her cheer. Everyone in the hospital loved her.

And then, during a minor operation, her heart had stopped on the table, and everybody just lost it.

Now there was a theological problem.

Hunt went to the funeral. Her pastor told all the mourners that it was okay to cry, okay to have tears. But they also had to have hope. We have to have hope.

I had hope, I thought, but their stories were scaring the crap out of me. I knew I could handle the academic part of seminary — I've been in college for the last twenty-five years, after all—but could I handle the pastoral things? CPE, my two-year field placement in some parish? And even though things had worked out miraculously for me to be here, was this really truly what I was supposed to be doing?

I think I started to feel like things might be okay during our first class day in new student orientation when we were discussing a book by Father Daniel Groody about border ministry, about the economic and political problems undocumented workers faced and the spiritual problems that grew out of their hard lives. New Testament scholar Cynthia Briggs-Kittredge was leading the discussion, and as she called on people around the room, they admitted that the reading had made them angry; they were surprised, outraged, disheartened.

I raised my hand, and Cynthia called on me. "I can see how the political situation makes the issue seem almost unsolvable," I said. "But reading the stories and hearing the voices of the people involved reminds me that this isn't an issue. It's about individuals. And maybe you can't help 'people.' But you can help a person. That gives me hope."

I paused and Cynthia turned to the class to get their reaction.

My own reaction was this: Hope?

Is that really me talking?

That night I sat with Roger on the front porch of his house as he waited for his date to arrive. I had brought over a six of cold Newcastle Brown Ale—I'd had a sneaking suspicion that he might be outside when I got home—and we sat and drank and talked. It was a warm night, and when I first sat down I sprayed myself—oversprayed, it quickly became clear from my stench—for mosquitoes.

I had never seen Roger so happy — so at peace. I knew that a week earlier, he had been formally admitted to postulancy in the Diocese of Arkansas, which meant that at long last the church was asking him to do what he'd been wanting to do all along, had at last admitted him into the ranks of the priests-to-be.

He told me he was working on a novel and told me about it, the story behind it, the real-life characters who inspired it. Roger had published a great book called *Running the Spiritual Path*, and I told him I'd love to see this book when he felt ready to show it to someone.

"I'm working on it every morning," he told me, and I could see that this was a story that animated him.

But that wasn't all.

"Greg," he said, and as he leaned forward in his lawn chair, I thought his smile might split his head wide open, "I think I'm in love."

And although I've had more than my share of hard luck and heartache and people are sometimes nervous about reporting their romantic happiness to me, I could tell that my smile was going to rival his.

"I'm glad to hear that," I said.

When she arrived, I could see by the way she ran up the front steps that she felt exactly the same way about him. So I told her how happy I was to meet her, and I gave Roger's arm a squeeze, and then I gathered my beer and got off the porch. They had better things to do than hang out with me.

"Good night," she called as I headed back toward my apartment.

"'Night, buddy," Roger said.

"Good night," I told them, and what I remember thinking was, *God bless*.

What I was thinking was that it is a good life after all.

What I was thinking was that I was going to be a person who lives in hope.

Now, I hadn't started orientation that way. The first day of orientation was devoted to what my friend Joe, a smart and funny guy from Kansas City, calls "sharing," as in, "If I'd known I was going to have to share, I'm not sure I would have come to this seminary."

We sat in the lobby or narthex of the chapel, all twenty-some of the incoming juniors, and heard the ground rules as the dean gave them. The person holding the candle would tell us—in three minutes, please—a story about what had brought them to ETSS. Then that person would pass the candle to another person to invite him or her to speak, and so on, until all of us had had the chance to talk a little about ourselves and our calling to seminary.

Some of the stories were amazing—there was Chris, talking about how he'd been diagnosed with full-blown AIDS, buried all his friends, and now wanted to minister to those suffering; there was Kevin, trained as an anthropologist, talking about how he'd come to believe in God against his will on an archaeological dig in the Middle East. And there was Arturo, who went so far over the three-minute limit that I thought I would need supplemental oxygen when at length I heard him say, "And then, in 1980—"

I was chosen next to last, and I had started to sweat. I would have been happy to go early, and going so near the end made me worry again that maybe I didn't really belong here.

The story I told was about Sarah Beth. Every semester at Baylor, students come to me with a problem, because for whatever reason they think that I'm the only one who will listen to them. Sometimes it's an unplanned pregnancy, sometimes an eating disorder, sometimes dangerous depression, sometimes substance abuse, sometimes a crisis of faith. And I know why they come, actually; they know that I've been hurt, that I've been broken, and that I can listen to them without judgment because I have been in whatever dark place they find themselves.

Sarah Beth came to me with a recurring problem that was killing her. It doesn't matter what it was, just that it was. I listened to her, I encouraged her to get help, and a few days later, her parents came to pull her out of school so that she could get treatment. I was so happy to know that she was going to get help, I was almost able to overlook how much I would miss having her around.

After her folks had checked her out of school and packed up her stuff, she begged them for the chance to come and sit in my class for one last time, to say good-bye to the other students, and they said okay. So there she sat in the front row, a new light on her face, listening to the discussion like it was the last time she'd ever hear people talk.

She had to drop out of school. But it saved her life.

When she was gone, she wrote from the treatment center to tell me that she was getting better. Every time I heard from her, I gave the class a report and asked them to remember Sarah Beth in their thoughts and prayers. I still remember her; I say her name every time we're given a chance to speak our prayers in chapel or during a service, because she's come to represent not only the wonderful and brave person that she is, but all of my students wrestling with God alone knows what problems lie behind those cheerful facades and fashionable clothes.

The world is full of broken people who think they're surrounded by whole people.

Saying her name is also a prayer of thanks that I could be a part of her trip toward healing and wholeness. I hope I can be part of that trip for many others, because I know what it's like to suffer and I know what it's like to be whole, and believe me, whole is a whole lot better.

When Greg and I had coffee a few months later at the Starbucks on Forty-fifth and Lamar — our typical meeting place — he asked me for a summary of the semester. "Tell me about your favorite student," he said, and I told him the story of Sarah Beth.

"So," he said after I finished, and he was smirking a little, because I was still playing Mr. I-don't-know-that-I'm-supposed-to-go-to-seminary, "so, what do you think it means that your favorite student actually dropped out halfway through the semester? Maybe there's more going on in your head than just teaching."

I wasn't going to give him the satisfaction, but he went where he wanted to go with it anyway. "You already do everything that I do," he said. "You preach, you teach, you do pastoral care. You can do this."

And that, I told the group, the candle in my hand, was why I was at seminary: Because I felt called to help people achieve wholeness the same way I'd been helped, through the church with a big "C" and a small "c," and because Greg and others like him had told me the church needed people like me to take the same ridiculous chance that they were all taking.

Although it was hard for me, I was conscious about getting to know people during orientation. Some people came up to engage me in conversation, like Jenny from Boston, who had read and been moved by my novel *Cycling* over the winter, "a time when I really needed it," she said. Others, I had to engage. But after a few days I could already tell that there were people in my class I could be good friends with, and shy or not, I decided that if I was going to work this hard and sacrifice this much, I wasn't going to hold myself back from any part of the two-week orientation experience.

That included the three-day retreat for members of the new class, which came after I had already started teaching the fall semester at Baylor. I had permission from Cynthia to miss some of the orientation sessions during my first week of classes at Baylor; I felt I really needed to be there to teach, because first classes set a tone. You can inspire someone to work hard and learn, or you can tell them that what you're doing isn't all that important.

I wanted my students to think of my classes as important, because I knew both of them — American literature and fiction writing — could be life changing, and they did turn out to be wonderful classes, as good as any I've ever taught.

The orientation retreat, though, would take me away during the second week, and although I made arrangements for my Baylor classes, I have to tell you that it felt very weird driving out to MO Ranch, the conference center in the Texas Hill Country where we'd be staying for three days.

I've taught class with a 102 degree temperature, I've taught class when I could barely manage to get myself out of bed, and if I'd wanted a test about whether I was supposed to be going to seminary, I could not have prepared a more potent one than having to miss class for it.

I drove out alone, although I knew that some of the folks were planning to carpool, since it was several hours away. I like driving, and I like driving alone, especially if it gives me a chance to listen to music and think and maybe jot a few words in my journal. I need lots and lots of alone time, and when you have a couple of different jobs including parenting, sometimes drive time is the only real alone time you can look forward to.

It was still plenty hot in late August, even as I drove up into the Hill Country west of Austin, but clouds were rolling in and it promised to cool off and maybe even rain. I had the windows of my latest ancient Volvo down and the sunroof open, and I was listening to Radiohead as I took the twists and turns through the hills and along the streams and rivers. At last, I followed the Guadalupe River to the gates of MO Ranch, drove inside, found the room I'd be sharing with De, and unloaded my bag, my guitar, and took a few things out of my backpack before shrugging it on.

Nobody else from the seminary was around yet, so I went out to wander among the trees and buildings. The ranch was big, with lots of room to ramble. I wandered down to the river's edge, where there was a giant slide with a kind of one-person toboggan you could ride out into the river, canoes piled along the bank, and a rope swing you could use to arc up and out over the water.

A light rain began to fall, just a sprinkle, as I decided to hike up the bluffs over the river to the highest part of the camp and then came back down a ways to the open-air chapel, still high over the river and looking off over the countryside. A rustic wood cross stood behind the stone pulpit, and semicircular stone benches were set into the hillside.

Back at Baylor, my fiction writing class was meeting without me, and some of my colleagues were probably questioning my sanity, not, I'm sure, for the first time.

I walked over to the cross, ran my fingertips across the rough grain, and said, out loud, "Okay. What am I doing here?"

I looked up at the cross, tried to imagine what message Jesus might give me if he were hanging there in truth.

What I got was an image of Jesus laughing, which was not a great help. A little too ambiguous for my tastes.

I raised my hand up to where his feet would be, felt the splinters there, wondered if I might be having a mystical moment.

Nope.

Then I sat down and took a good long drink from my water bottle as the rain fell gently on my head.

"If you drink this water you will thirst again," I remember Jesus saying. "But I will give you living water."

Oh, I thought to myself.

Okay.

I opened my Bible to the gospel of Mark, took a look at the next chapter I would have to retell for the Bible project that Chris and I were working on. It was Mark 12, where Jesus sends out the Twelve and commissions them to travel light, to anoint the sick, to heal.

Okay, I thought. The divine Sam I Am is in the house.

I got up, and instead of following the road back down to the river, I decided to cross the long and high metal bridge over the ravine. It was made of oilfield pipes, it looked like, and iron grating, and when you stepped out onto it, you could see straight through the grating to the ground about sixty feet below.

Now I am not so fond of heights, and although I could see the grating, it was like it wasn't there. The far-off ground assumed an importance in my thoughts it should not have had.

And then, I don't know whether I was talking to myself or someone else was talking to me, but I swear to you, I heard these words in my head:

Look straight ahead.
Don't look down.
Trust that there's something holding you up.

So I did. I walked all the way across the bridge and back up to the lodge, and people were just starting to arrive, and I waved at them, shyly.

Now it amazes me to think that there was ever a time in my life when I didn't know these people, but then we were still getting to know each other, and that retreat changed things.

We worked. I was one of three people who had brought a guitar, and I played for worship for the first time in a good twenty years, and it felt good. We talked together in small groups — team-building stuff. We watched the John Sayles movie *Lone Star*, and the next morning we talked about the political and theological issues it brought up for us about life on the border — which is what Texas is, of course.

We played. On our free afternoon, Heath, one of the Lutheran seminarians, and I carried the heavy wooden sled up the slide and went down it and out into the river, over and over. It was exhilarating, if, the first time, terrifying. One of the great pleasures that afternoon was watching people making their first run, like the dean of the seminary, whose face bore a look of abject terror mingled with joy. On my final run of the day, I hit the water just exactly so, my balance was perfect, and I shot out into the river to the last buoy like a flat rock skipping, farther than anyone else had gone all day, and I swam back to the accompaniment of applause and cheering from the bank.

In impromptu guitar pulls at night, I played Beatles songs and some of my own songs, and Steven, another of the Lutherans, and I started a do-it-yourself blues we called "The Seminary Blues," to which anyone could add a verse.

After lights out, we stayed up together in small groups and drank and talked quietly in the dark, like kids at camp.

And we listened. Charlie Cook, who like Cynthia was one of the professors that Roger and Hunt loved dearly, preached at our retreat Eucharist. His homily was about the call — about how most of the calls in the Bible — to Moses, to Paul, to whomever — hadn't made sense to the people receiving them. Many of them didn't even want to receive a call. And that, he said, was probably good, their not jumping up and down about God asking them to do something.

"To be too sure of yourself is a bad thing," he said in that inimitable drawl of his.

Charlie's words were the last piece of the puzzle for me. Despite everything that had happened to me along the way, all the messages, the billboards and skywriting, as well as the subliminal things nobody but me might have noticed, despite all the urgings of the divine Sam I Am, I still had come into orientation not very sure of myself. I don't think you can expect to run from religion your whole adult life, make fun of devout Christians for twenty years, and then look up to discover that you're studying for the priesthood without a good chunk of cognitive dissonance.

It certainly had me shaking my head at the freakiness of life.

But those three days were exactly what I needed — the messages, the involvement, the community, the affirmations — to finally convince me that I was where I belonged.

On the afternoon of the third day, as we all reluctantly prepared to head back to Austin, I decided to turn right at the ranch entrance instead of left, the way everyone else was going back to Austin. A little more driving would be good for me, I thought, and I wasn't quite ready to let go of the experience yet.

The sun was shining, I had the windows down and the sunroof open, and the first song on Radiohead's *OK Computer* was playing.

And as I made the turn, I heard twice in the first verse the line "I am born again," and a huge smile spread across my face.

"Yeah," I said. "Yeah. That seems about right."

And then off I drove, in my own roundabout way, swooping and soaring through the Hill Country on the way back to my brand-new life.

walking around in the light

God of our weary years, God of our silent tears,
Thou who hast brought us thus far on the way,
Thou who hast by thy might led us into the light,
Keep us forever in the path we pray.

JAMES WELDON JOHNSON, "LIFT EVERY VOICE AND SING"

That rainy afternoon when I walked across that so-called bridge at MO Ranch was almost a year ago as I write this. A few months back, in May, I took Chandler back to MO Ranch with Ken and Joe and Don and their families, and we spent the day picnicking and swimming and playing, and the closed circle began to have a look of completion to it.

It was again a beautiful drive out into the Hill Country, the Texas wildflowers coloring the highways and country roads. As I floated in the Guadalupe River and occasionally climbed the thirty-foot tall slide to launch myself across the river, I felt a sense of peace and certainty I've rarely known — the sense that I was in the right place at the right time doing the right thing.

Although it has been a challenging year and my fate as a possible ordained leader in the Episcopal Church is still up in the air, I have no doubt that seminary is where God wants me to be.

It has been a year of signs and symbols.

Last summer, before I started seminary, I was in the Sangre de Cristos again, camped at the trailhead of the Trampas River, and after the always-challenging end-of-the-year at Baylor, the end of suspense over my admission to seminary, and my work finishing a book on religion and comic books, I was ready to be alone in nature again.

Or so I thought. As always, when I left Austin it was boiling hot, and when I arrived in the Trampas Valley it was chilly. I slept that night in a sweatshirt and ski hat, and still woke up the next morning shivering as the sun rose over the mountains.

I cautiously opened my sleeping bag and was hit by a blast of cold air. *No thanks*, I thought. I pulled the bag up over my head and just lay there shivering for a while.

But the light was insistent. I could lie there in my tent, shivering, and say I'd seen it, Okay, Mom, I'm up, or I could get out and walk in it, and I knew that hard as it might be at this moment, when I did it, it would feel good.

As I pulled clothes on and shivered some more, I found that I had one of my favorite songs from St. James going through my head: "We Are Marching in the Light of God." I've heard it sung at other places, even in the seminary chapel, but it often sounds like a funeral march instead of the upbeat way it should be sung. The three verses have the same words — just in three difference languages, English, Spanish, and Zulu — and really the words are just the joyful repetition of the phrase "We are marching in the light of God."

I can tell you from New Testament Greek that the author of

the epistles of John in the Christian Testament thought that the image of walking was the best metaphor for the life of faith. The Greek word he used was *peripateo* (περιπατεο), and although at this moment I am sitting at Trampas Lake again, over 11,000 feet above sea level and 600 miles from my Greek dictionary, the seminary has taught me well. When John writes of his delight in discovering that church members are walking in truth, he uses this word, and what I love about it is that it doesn't just mean "walking." It actually means "walking around." So it's not necessarily about walking in a straight line, following a straight-forward path, but it is about walking continuously, walking without stopping.

It has been a year since I last camped here and hiked up to these lakes, and as I said, it has been a year of signs and symbols. Last year, after I'd managed to get out of my cold tent and on the trail, I strode right past the point where I usually sat and took my first rest in pursuit of the elusive element oxygen. In fact, I was well into the hike, two miles or so, before I began to notice that my footing seemed uncertain. There were no stumbling stones beneath my feet—the σξανδαλον I taught you about—and yet I seemed to be sliding with every step I took.

Since I'm not completely incapable of everyday life, when I heard a flapping noise coming from the direction of my feet, I sat down on a fallen tree and took a closer look. What I saw actually freaked me out a little, and not just because I was a couple of miles into a hard hike and it was a little late for things to go wrong with my equipment.

It didn't take even a close look to see that the thick Vibram sole was falling off my right hiking boot.

Not just a little—it had peeled all the way back to the heel so that the bottom of my boot looked like a crocodile's smile. And when I raised my foot up to take a closer look, the whole sole just fell off, plop, into the dusty path.

Okay. Weird enough. But when I looked at the other boot, the same thing was happening — the left sole was also about to fall completely off my boot.

Now I'm sure I don't have to tell you that if I'd noticed the soles falling off my boots back in camp, I would never have set out on a monster hike with them on.

So I think it would be safe to say that I was a little stunned.

I'd had those boots for ten years. They were expensive Merrill boots, heavy and high and waterproof. I'd bought them originally because I'd always had weak ankles and I thought I needed the protection.

Those boots had done more than carry me through the Wind River Range and the backcountry of Glacier National Park. They'd also carried me through some of the only peaceful moments I'd had in some of the hardest years of my life. Although they were ten years old, I only wore them a few times a year, and they'd always been stored, clean and dry, in the back of my closet.

So what, we wonder, is the universe trying to say when it up and decides that suddenly you can't walk another mile on this path in your old shoes?

Well, maybe just that, I thought. Maybe my old shoes were a symbol of my beat-up old life. It was Thoreau who said we shouldn't put on new clothes until we ourselves had changed, so that wearing the old ones felt false and arbitrary, like keeping new wine in old bottles, to use Jesus' illustration. "Our moulting season," Thoreau said, "must be a crisis in our lives."[1]

Or maybe it meant that I didn't need these clunky high boots anymore. Maybe it was time to trust that something or someone else could keep me from falling, from hurting myself.

And maybe it meant that my shoes picked that particular moment to self-destruct, in stereo, but you know, I just don't think so.

Since I'm a writer, I live in a world of metaphor and symbol, and when on a morning that I'm humming a song about walking in the light of God my old shoes fall off my feet as I'm hiking in the sunlight, you can bet that I'm going to see it as a symbol.

Maybe it wasn't, as Jules would say in *Pulp Fiction*, an according to Hoyle miracle. But all the same, I felt the touch of God.

God got involved.

So I pulled my trusty Teva sandals out of my backpack and put them on my feet, shouldered my pack, and went on my way. And I didn't stumble, and I didn't turn my ankle, and I arrived here at Trampas Lake with that elusive sense of peace and certainty that I mentioned earlier. Something strange had just happened, true—but then, what about my life has ever been normal?

Evangelical Christians sometimes talk about their walk with the Lord just as the writer of John did, and other folks talk about the journey of faith, because walking is a metaphor that works. Even if you believe, as many people do, that the life of faith centers around a single fateful decision—"Have you accepted Jesus Christ as your personal Lord and Savior?"—the life of faith doesn't end there. Another of my favorite Baptist hymns says, "I have decided to follow Jesus." It's a decision and following both, the walking around in Christ's footsteps.

It's what Maya Angelou told me some years ago back at Baylor: "I'm not a Christian," she said. "I am *trying* to be a

Christian." I think the distinction is important. Too many Christians think that the decision, which in their thinking determines whether you spend eternity in heaven or hell, is enough — that, maybe, and helping out on Wednesday nights with dinner in the fellowship hall or teaching vacation Bible school. But the only Christian life that makes sense to me is continuously walking in the light of God — walking around in the footsteps of Jesus.

Earlier today, after I crossed over the river for the first time far back near the beginning of the valley, a long time and a lot of altitude ago, I stopped for a second and looked at the ridgeline ahead of me, facing the choice that I make whenever I hike this trail.

There have been a few times — not for a while now, so don't yell at me, but there have been times — when I've left the trail behind, clambered to the top of the mountains, pulling myself up by trees and rocks and roots, puffing and scrambling until I reach the top, about 12,000 feet or so. Then I walk the length of the valley up on top of the mountains, around to the far end of the lakes, where I find an avalanche chute of some kind and climb down to make the return trip on the trail.

Climbing down is much harder than climbing up, which is hard enough.

It is not a technical climb — that is, you don't need ropes and special equipment to make it — but it is a dangerous one, with plenty of chances to fall hundreds of feet to your death and that sort of thing.

Since I have almost always made this hike alone, I always made the climb alone, despite the danger, despite the fact that if something happened to me, no one would ever know what happened to me.

I never thought about the danger, anymore than I thought about the danger of stepping in front of a bus that summer five years ago in Santa Fe. Unlike that afternoon, I wasn't explicitly trying to kill myself. But I can say that I didn't care much what happened to me in those days, so why not climb a mountain?

I stood there this morning, thinking about the mountain goats up on top, about the views — hundreds of miles in every direction — about the incredible feeling of accomplishment. I stood there, and I thought about all the things that have changed in my life — so much more than the new hiking shoes I have on now — and all of a sudden, those things came together in a moment of decision.

It was tempting. I knew the climb would be thrilling. I knew the view from the top would be unmatched.

But I smiled, shook my head, walked on, crossed the river for the second time, and trudged on up the trail.

I told the mountain I couldn't climb it because I had a book to finish, a book that somebody out there might need to read. But what I was really saying — what I've accepted as a story worth living and dying for — is that God saved me five years ago for a reason, and I'm not going to do anything stupid now that I know what direction I'm headed.

As I walk around in my different shoes, marching in the light of God, do I think that two years from now when I complete seminary, I'll be ordained as an Episcopal priest?

I don't know. And you know, it almost doesn't matter. What I do know is that as long as I have life and breath, I'm going to try to be a Christian. I'm going to write and teach and preach and live in a fashion that shows how thankful I am for the life that I once wanted to end.

I'm going to try to be the healing hands of Christ in a broken and hurting world.

That's all I know.

And really, that matters more than anything else, any title you could put in front of my name, any collar you could put around my neck.

Those big dark clouds rolling in now from the southwest — and these mosquitoes that either found me or followed me from down below — are reminding me that it's time to get to my feet and walk on, that as beautiful as the Trampas Lake is, as important to me as it has been, it isn't a final destination.

It's a good lesson — life is full of things we think are destinations, when really they're only rest stops.

There's no straight path from the shore of the lake where I sit, mosquito-gnawed, back to the beginning of the trail heading down the mountain. Almost always I have to blunder around, wading through mud, climbing over fallen trees, before striking where I'm supposed to be.

But I don't worry about that anymore, because — although it's taken me my whole life — I've learned two important things. First, if you know the general direction you're headed — and I do — you don't have to know the exact path. And if you believe that God can make straight things out of crooked — and I do — then blundering around is never in vain. In fact, oftentimes it will take you exactly where you're supposed to go.

So now I'm going to change my socks — because sometimes you can't go another mile in your old socks — and take up my heavy pack, and I'm going to walk back down the mountain.

And I know that God will follow me all the way back down the mountain, and later, when the time comes, all the way back home.

author's note

When you're writing a book about your life, there's a lot you have to leave out, and just because I left something out of this book doesn't mean it's not plenty important. There are very important things, like my sons, my teaching, my music, and my love of movies and pop culture, among others, that could have gotten a whole lot more space in another book about my life. It's just that they were peripheral in some ways to the main story of this one, which is about depression and faith. My love for my boys, Jake and Chandler, permeates this book, even if they're not always center stage. Thanks, guys, for the honor and pleasure of being your dad.

I chose to use initials instead of the actual names of some of the folks involved in this story because I wanted, at least as far as I could, to safeguard their privacy. I have set out here to tell you some of my secrets in the service of this story; I have striven not to tell anyone else's secrets. I want to acknowledge Tinamarie, who shared many of these bad times and who nevertheless forgave me for them. And there were many good times as well that continue into the now, where we share parenting for a wonderful boy. I don't want the focus of the book to suggest that ours was not a loving relationship; I hope what I've written shows that losing something that mattered so much to me was one of the things that pushed me over the edge.

I've also tried to be as true to the story as I can. There are a few places where I've condensed events a little to simplify the narrative (as Thoreau did in *Walden*, squeezing two years into one), but I have never changed an outcome, emotion, or conclusion, to the best of my knowledge. Depression, insomnia, and antidepressants all may have affected my recall, and there is much about the years I write about that I not only can't remember but don't want to remember. But everything I've related here is the "happening truth" as I understand it. Of course, different people may have different memories about events, but these are mine.

I'm grateful to the good people at NavPress who asked me to think about writing this book long before there was a book to write. Their belief that I could pull the scattered events of my eventful life together into something worth reading encouraged me to think about how I might do that, and this book is here in large part because they believed I could write it. I've enjoyed every book we've done together. I want to express my thanks to everyone I've worked with at NavPress and Piñon Press for the beautiful book covers and design, advertising and sales support, and constant enthusiasm. Gracias to publisher Dan Rich, editorial director Terry Behimer, marketing and publicity gurus Mike Kennedy and Andrea Christian, respectively, my editor Don Simpson, and, especially, my editor Steve Parolini, who had a vision for this book. God bless you all for your good work. May it bear rich fruit.

I was also encouraged to write this book by my friend Greg Rickel and the members of my parish, St. James Episcopal in Austin, Texas; by many people at the Episcopal Seminary of the

Southwest, particularly my teachers, my classmates Lisa Miller, Don Smith, Joe Behen, Kevin Schubert, De Freeman, Heath Abel, and Ken Malcolm, and graduated but never forgotten seminarians Hunt Priest, Roger Joslin, and Liz Muñoz.

My friend and fellow writer the Rev. Scott Walker told me years ago I should write this book. Well, Scott, here it is, and thanks for all the help and support you've given me over the years. Chris Seay kept me alive, loved me without reserve, fed my body whenever I came around, and gave me projects to work on with him that fed my soul as well. Thanks, Buddy. My spiritual director, Joe Barry, heard me talk about some of these things and helped me to clarity about many of them. And Rebecca Taylor provided support, affection, and inspiration during the writing of this book in exchange for backrubs; I think I got the better end of that deal.

I've had wonderful models for this kind of spiritual writing in the works of Anne Lamott, Dennis Covington, and Kathleen Norris, and in nonfiction works for the emerging church by Lauren Winner, Don Miller, Chris Seay, and Brian McLaren. Thanks, all, for your honesty, your commitment to craft, and your faithfulness to God. I'm also a lover of the prose of Thomas Merton and Martin Luther King, and the nonfiction of Walker Percy, and trust their influence on me has made me better at what I've tried to do here. If any of these writers are new to you and you enjoyed this book, then please track them down. You won't be sorry.

Toward the end of the writing of this book, I was fortunate enough to have an internship at Ghost Ranch-Santa Fe and to be teaching a class at Ghost Ranch in Abiquiu, where I have done some of my very best writing. Special thanks to Jim Baird for giving me the opportunity and for hosting me with his usual kindness.

I wrote this book during a research leave granted by Baylor University in the spring and summer of 2005. I'm grateful to then-Provost David Lyle Jeffrey, current Provost Randall O'Brien, my dean Wallace Daniel, my chair Maurice Hunt, and to my colleagues in the Department of English for taking up some of the slack while I was goner than usual. Thanks also to my students, all of whom I love and gladly serve. If these stories help one of them, then this excavation in the dark cellars of my soul has not been in vain.

I listened to Coldplay, Keane, Bob Schneider, Radiohead, Bruce Springsteen, and Bruce Hornsby while I wrote this book, and to Coldplay's X & Y as I edited it. Thanks to all these great artists for comfort and inspiration.

Greg Garrett plays Yamaha guitars, Roland amps, Martin strings, and Hohner harmonicas.

Five years ago, I didn't expect to be alive today — or to want to be alive. This book is an offering of thanks to God, Creator, Redeemer, and Sustainer, for life and breath and the opportunity to make a difference in the world.

Grace and peace,
Greg Garrett
August 2005
Austin, Texas

NOTES

Last Rites
1. Frank Griswold, accessed at http://www.episcopalchurch.org/1275_1312_ENG _HTM.htm.

Prayers for the Departed
1. Rob Brezhny, accessed at www.austinchronicle.com July 17, 2004.

Family History
1. Anne Lamott, *Traveling Mercies: Some Thoughts on Faith* (New York: Anchor, 1999), 193.

Direction
1. Parker Palmer, *Let Your Life Speak* (San Francisco: Jossey-Bass, 2000), 57.
2. Walker Percy, "The Man on the Train," *The Message in the Bottle*, 1975 (New York: Picador, 2000), 83.
3. Anne Lamott, *Traveling Mercies: Some Thoughts on Faith* (New York: Anchor, 1999), 107.

Solitude
1. Thomas Merton, *The Wisdom of the Desert*, 1960 (New York: New Directions, 1970), 6-7.
2. Henry David Thoreau, *Walden and Civil Disobedience*, 1854 (New York: Penguin, 1986), 135.
3. Matthew 11:28-31, ASV.
4. William Sloane Coffin, *Credo* (Louisville, KY: Westminster/John Knox, 2004), 8-9.

Martin
1. Martin Luther King Jr., "Letter from a Birmingham Jail," *I Have a Dream* (New York: Harper SanFrancisco, 1992), 96.
2. William Sloane Coffin, *Credo* (Louisville, KY: Westminster/John Knox, 2004), 57.
3. King, 92.
4. Henri Nouwen, *The Wounded Healer* (New York: Image, 1972), 93.

Writing
1. Anne Lamott, *Traveling Mercies: Some Thoughts on Faith* (New York: Anchor, 1999), 61.
2. Shelby Foote and Walker Percy, *The Correspondence of Shelby Foote and Walker Percy*, ed. Jay Tolson (New York: Norton, 1996), 64.
3. Thomas Merton, *New Seeds of Contemplation*, 1961 (Boston: Shambhala, 2003), 113.
4. Walker Percy, "Notes for a Novel About the End of the World," *The Message in the Bottle*, 1975 (New York: Picador, 2000), 111.
5. Thomas Merton, *Conjectures of a Guilty Bystander*, 1968 (New York: Image, 1989), 92.

In the Valley
1. J. Philip Newell, *Listening for the Heartbeat of God: A Celtic Spirituality* (New York: Paulist, 1997), 14.
2. Urban Holmes, *What Is Anglicanism?* (Harrisburg, PA: Morehouse, 1982), 27.

Simplicity
1. Jim Wallis, *God's Politics: Why the Right Gets It Wrong and the Left Doesn't Get It* (New York: HarperSanFrancisco, 2005), 72.
2. Thomas Merton, *Conjectures of a Guilty Bystander*, 1968 (New York: Image, 1989), 98.
3. Thomas Moore, "Introduction," Thomas Merton, *Conjectures of a Guilty Bystander*, 1968 (New York: Image, 1989), vii.
4. Wallis, 5.
5. Henry David Thoreau, *Walden and Civil Disobedience*, 1854 (New York: Penguin, 1983), 135.
6. Accessed at http://www.houstonprogressive.org/hpn/nlc-swsh.html.

Sin
1. Thomas Merton, *No Man Is an Island*, 1955 (New York: Harcourt, 1983), 10-11.
2. Anne Lamott, *Traveling Mercies: Some Thoughts on Faith* (New York: Anchor, 1999), 254-255.

Neighbors
1. Anne Lamott, *Traveling Mercies: Some Thoughts on Faith* (New York: Anchor, 1999), 134.
2. Martin Luther King Jr., "I See the Promised Land," *I Have a Dream* (New York: HarperSanFrancisco, 1992), 201.

Credo
1. Karen Armstrong, *A History of God* (New York: Ballantine, 1993), 111.
2. Kathleen Norris, *Amazing Grace: A Vocabulary of Faith* (New York: Riverhead, 1998), 64-66.
3. Lauren Winner, *Girl Meets God* (New York: Random House, 2002), 269.
4. The Dalai Lama, *Ethics for the New Millennium* (New York: Riverhead, 1999), 228.
5. John 15:12, KJV.

Obedience
1. Bruce Feiler, *Walking the Bible: A Journey by Land Through the Five Books of Moses* (New York: Perennial, 2002), 91.
2. Romans 6:16, NRSV.
3. Bruce Feiler, *Abraham: A Journey to the Heart of Three Faiths* (New York: Perennial, 2004), 96-97.
4. Feiler, *Abraham*, 104.
5. Matthew 10:37-39, NRSV.
6. Burton L. Mack, *Who Wrote the New Testament?: The Making of the Christian Myth* (New York: HarperSanFrancisco, 1995), 87.
7. Corinne Ware, *Saint Benedict on the Freeway: A Rule of Life for the 21st Century* (Nashville: Abingdon, 2001), 29.

Walking Around in the Light

1. Henry David Thoreau, *Walden and Civil Disobedience*, 1854 (New York: Penguin, 1983), 66.

MORE HONEST AND CHALLENGING BOOKS FROM NAVPRESS.

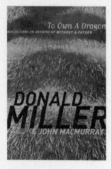